KILLINGS

Calvin Trillin

KILLINGS

TICKNOR & FIELDS

NEW YORK

The pieces in this book first appeared in *The New Yorker*.

Library of Congress Cataloging in Publication Data

Trillin, Calvin.
Killings.

1. Murders—United States—Addresses, essays,
lectures.   I. Title.
HV6529.T74   1984   364.1′523′0973   83-9313
ISBN 0-89919-233-5

Printed in the United States of America

S 10 9 8 7 6 5 4 3 2

To the *New Yorker* reporter who set
the standard — Joseph Mitchell

Contents

· v i i ·

Contents

Introduction

Reporters love murders. In a pinch, what the lawyers call "wrongful death" will do, particularly if it's sudden. Even a fatal accident for which no one is to blame has some appeal. On a daily newspaper, in fact, an accident is one of the few news events whose importance can be precisely measured by the editors who decide how much space and prominence each story is worth. In general, the space it is assigned varies directly with how many people were killed — assuming, of course, that they were not Orientals. Sufficient loss of life can elevate an accident story into a category of news that is almost automatically front-page — a disaster.

I have always been attracted by stories of sudden death. For fifteen years, starting in the fall of 1967, I traveled around the United States to do a series of reporting pieces for *The New Yorker* called "U.S. Journal" — an article every three weeks from somewhere in the country — and once or twice every year I found myself at the scene of a killing. What attracted me was not importance as a newspaper editor might measure it — the number of people killed, for instance, or how closely they resembled the readers ("According to airline officials in New Delhi, there were no Americans aboard the plane"), or the prominence of the victim in the community or in the nation. A magazine like *The New Yorker* does not have the record-keeping function that a newspaper has. If a federal judge is assassinated in Texas or twelve people are killed by floods in the West, *The New Yorker* is not responsible for registering the event for the record. By the same token, it can — and did in some of these pieces — record the death of a single unimportant person without feeling the need to justify its interest the way a newspaper might ("The Iowa murder is part of a growing national trend toward vaguely disreputable people in small towns killing each other").

While I was in the South working on one of the stories in this book, I happened to meet some reporters for the local newspaper, and they couldn't imagine why I had come all the way from New York to write about a death that probably hadn't even made their front page. Only one person had died, and she had not been an important person. Her family was not particularly important, and neither was the person accused of causing her death. The way she had died did not reflect any national trends. Her death had been the central event in what struck me as a remarkable family drama, but it seemed trivialized by the old newspaper phrase used to describe such dramas — a human-interest story. The best I could manage was "It sounded interesting."

I often wished that I could come up with something grander than that, particularly when I was asked by relatives of some victim why I was pursuing a subject that caused them pain to discuss. Not having to justify your interest is a great luxury for a reporter, but it is also a small burden. At times, I would have welcomed the opportunity to say "The public has a right to know" or "This story could prevent this sort of thing from happening again." I couldn't even claim that I was an innocent party who had been assigned the story by the callous city editor of newspaper legend ("Hey, champ, get on your roller skates and get out to Laurel Avenue and talk to this lady whose husband just shot himself — and don't come back without their wedding picture"). I chose the stories for "U.S. Journal" myself, mostly on the basis of what sounded interesting.

What I was interested in, of course, was writing about America — or, as I realized a few years after I began "U.S. Journal," in writing about America without an emphasis on politics and government. Some ways of doing that didn't suit my needs. I wasn't interested in doing what is sometimes called Americana — stories about people like the last fellow in Jasper County, Georgia, who can whittle worth a damn. I didn't want to do stories about typical or representative Americans — stories about, say, the struggles of A Midwestern Farm Family to make ends meet. Although I was interested in places, I wasn't comfortable writing about a city or a state or a region in general terms; I didn't do stories that could be called "Boston at Three Hundred" or "Is the New South Really New?" I went every three weeks not to a place but to a story — to an event or a controversy or, now and then, a killing.

A killing often seemed to present the best opportunity to write about people one at a time. There were occasions, of course, when I found myself treating a killing as an element in a controversy that involved blocs of people rather than individuals. I once did a piece in Seattle after a white policeman had shot and killed a black armed-robbery suspect: in the controversy that followed the shooting, they both became so enveloped by their roles that the incident could have been described in just that way — a White Cop had killed a Black Suspect. There were occasions when not knowing the identity of someone involved in a killing meant writing about a sort of person rather than a person — the sort of person who might get killed that way or the sort of person who might do the killing. Once, in the early seventies, I went to the West Coast of Florida to do a piece that involved efforts by the authorities — futile efforts, as it turned out — to learn the identity of a body that had been found in a trunk left in the woods next to a restaurant on the Interstate. The body was that of a twenty-five- to thirty-five-year-old woman. She had bad teeth. She had no scars. She had a bolo tie pulled tight around her throat. It turned out that a lot of twenty-five- to thirty-five-year-old women were considered missing by someone. In the first few days after the trunk was discovered, fifty people called the St. Petersburg Police Department to say that they thought they knew who the dead woman might have been. A man in his late forties phoned from central Florida to say that he thought the woman in the trunk was his wife, who had run off, with several hundred dollars of his money, in the company of a man in his thirties who drove a truck for a fruit company. A woman in Tampa said that her daughter had left home on October 28th — wearing a white blouse, pink pants, and green "flip-flops" — and had not been in touch since, although it had been said that she met some men in a bar in Tampa and went with them to the dog races in St. Petersburg. A twenty-six-year-old woman had been missing from Wimauma, Florida, ever since her father threatened two men who had been staying with her. A man in St. Petersburg phoned to say that the woman in the trunk might be the daughter he had thrown out of the house three months before. She had been carrying on with several different men while her husband was in Vietnam, the father said, and only the intervention of his wife had kept him from killing her himself on the day he threw her out. The man became so angry talking about what he would do if he ever got his hands on his daughter that he had to be warned that he could be considered a suspect and that anything he said might be used against him.

The reports called into the St. Petersburg Police Department conjured up a composite of a woman who might be the victim any time an unidentified body is discovered on the West Coast of Florida. She used to work as a cocktail waitress at a place called the Pink Panther or as a go-go dancer in a place out at the beach called Eddie's Seaview Lounge. She has a couple of children, but the children have been left with an ex-husband or with her mother up north. The ex-husband has threatened her. She runs around with kind of a wild crowd.

The stories of sudden death that most interested me, though, were not those in which the people involved could be thought of as a type of person or a representative of what the lawyers call "others so situated" — any itinerant cocktail waitress or any black suspect killed by a white policeman. When someone dies suddenly shades are drawn up, and the specificity of what is revealed was part of what attracted me. In London, in the summer of 1970, I accompanied an employee of the American consulate to a drab hotel room in Paddington where he had to collect the possessions of an American who had died suddenly, without any known relatives or friends in the area. The man had left nothing in the hotel room except the contents of a couple of cheap suitcases, some half-eaten sweet-rolls, and three empty Coca-Cola bottles near the bed. At the embassy, an inventory was taken. There was twenty-one dollars in cash. There was an old membership card in the Screen Actors Guild. There was an outdated passport, issued in the fifties, listing the man's occupation as car salesman. There was a letter, dated

1961, from an M-G-M executive in New York: the
executive said he was sorry to hear about the man's
having been under the weather and regretted that he
couldn't provide the World Series tickets the man was
looking for. There was another letter, dated 1968, from
a Las Vegas men's store telling whomever it might
concern that the man had been a courteous and responsible employee and had been let go only because
of a business slowdown. There was a card indicating
graduation from a bartender's school in Los Angeles
in 1968. There was a form letter from the governor of
Louisiana expressing appreciation for the interest
shown in investment opportunities in that state. There
were a lot of disposable syringes and an insulin bottle.
There were a couple dozen boxes of false eyelashes and
an invoice listing their wholesale and retail prices and
some Commerce Department booklets on how to set
up small export businesses. The inventory, of course,
provided some hints as to how the man had come to
be alone in that dreary hotel room, with a supply of
both insulin and Coca-Cola. It also provided me with
another reminder of the appeal sudden death has for
reporters: it gives us an excuse to be there, poking
around in somebody's life.

Reporters also tend to love trials. It may be that we
are transfixed by a process in which the person being
asked a question actually has to answer it. He cannot
say he would rather not comment. He cannot tell an
anecdote on a different subject. He has to answer the

question — under oath that he is telling the truth. I associate trials with killings. I think of a trial as one of the principal illumination devices switched on by sudden death. I suppose I carry around a kind of composite murder trial in my mind, along with a composite trunk-murder victim. The prosecutor is a cautious young man — an assistant district attorney — who wears wing-tip shoes and works methodically out of a loose-leaf notebook. The defense attorney is a bit flashier, and perhaps indiscreet enough to hint to reporters that his client is, in fact, guilty — the assumption being that a defense attorney who wins acquittal for a guilty client must be particularly brilliant. A defense lawyer can afford the style of a man not haunted by the prospect of having a victory reversed on appeal; there being no appeal from Not Guilty, he only has to win once. The caution of an assistant district attorney comes not only from the danger of reversible error but also from the conditions of his employment: a defense lawyer is engaged in private enterprise and an assistant district attorney is a man who works for the government.

Of course, I've been to a lot of trials in which the lawyers didn't fit my composites — Daniel Boone Smith, the commonwealth's attorney of Harlan County, Kentucky, was nothing at all like a cautious assistant D.A. — and a lot of trials that were not particularly illuminating. Over the years, I spent a lot of courtroom hours wishing the testimony would move away from bullet trajectory and toward some accounts of how the victim liked to spend his time or some speculation on why the defendant might have wanted him out of the way. Even so, I remain fascinated by trials. I even like the examination of the jury. In fact, I particularly like the examination of the jury. When I'm in a public place among strangers — on a bus, say, or in an airplane — I sometimes have a sudden urge to make an announcement: "All right, we're going to go right down this aisle and have everyone state his name and address and occupation and then answer a few questions I have about your immediate family and your background and your prejudices." In jury selection, that actually happens — and everybody is under oath to tell the truth.

The techniques of jury selection vary widely from place to place. In Eastern Kentucky, the jury-picking method of Daniel Boone Smith leaned heavily on what he knew about most of the families in the county — including how they felt about each other. In Brooklyn, I once sat through jury selection on a wrongful-death case with a plaintiff's lawyer whose strategy was based partly on a kind of informal ethnic sociology. The victim was a young woman — a thirty-two-year-old college teacher who had been killed in an auto accident. The lawyer for her family was looking for jurors who might be expected to place a high value on the life that was lost. To some extent, he was hoping for a personality type that he could describe only vaguely — open rather than closed, warm rather than cold. In another sense, though, he had his perfect juror specifically in mind: a fairly well-educated Jewish male in his sixties who had sent two or three children through college.

Obviously, an interest in the ways that thoroughly American places like Brooklyn and Harlan County differ was one reason I started on my travels. In these stories, the place was the context for the killing, and the killing was an opportunity to write about the place. I like to read murder mysteries — I believe the well-executed 175-page paperback murder mystery was put on earth to lighten the load of the traveling man flying between two American cities — and the ones I find absorbing are those that evoke a specific place. I'm more interested in what life is like in a Boston hospital or on the Navajo reservation or in South Africa than I am in who done it. The pieces in this book are nonfictional whodunits only in the sense that they are concerned with setting. Writing about, say, the murder of a prominent Miami criminal lawyer seemed to me inseparable from writing about the high life in south Florida.

At times during my travels, I may have become more interested in the community where the killing took place — or at least in the effect the killing had on the community — than I was in the victim. I was never much interested in the violence involved. Only a couple of these stories go into much detail about how someone was killed. This is not a book about the level of violence in America, except insofar that in this country a large selection of sudden deaths is taken for granted by a reporter looking for a story; I suppose someone doing "British Journal" or "Swedish Journal" would have to find another excuse for his presence. These stories are meant to be more about how Americans live than about how some of them die. If the old newspaper phrase didn't bring to mind an item about a motherly cocker spaniel adopting orphaned ducklings, I would be comfortable with calling them human-interest stories. Their appeal was that they were about specific humans, and I chose them, of course, because they sounded interesting.

Author's Note

I am grateful to William Shawn, the editor of *The New Yorker,* for encouraging the "U.S. Journal" series. I am also grateful to the late Robert Bingham, who edited most of these pieces, and to the other *New Yorker* manuscript editors and fact checkers who, week after week, did their level best to keep me from embarrassing myself.

Except for some minor corrections, the stories in this book are printed as they appeared in *The New Yorker.* They appear in chronological order and in the tense they were written in because I think their settings include the times as well as the place. Later developments that significantly changed stories are discussed in an Afterword at the end of the book.

These stories are obviously not meant to reflect a statistically balanced picture of how or where Americans meet sudden death. There is no story about a storekeeper killed during an armed robbery. There is no story about a carload of teenagers wiped out by a drunken driver. There are three stories that take place in Iowa. As it happens, I have always thought of Iowa as a relatively peaceful and particularly humane state — all in all, an unlikely place for a killing.

KILLINGS

A Stranger
with a Camera

Jeremiah, Kentucky
April 1969

ON A BRIGHT AFTERNOON in September, in 1967, a
five-man film crew working in the mountains of Eastern
Kentucky stopped to take pictures of some people near
a place called Jeremiah. In a narrow valley, a half-
dozen dilapidated shacks — each one a tiny square
box with one corner cut away to provide a cluttered
front porch — stood alongside the county blacktop.
Across the road from the shacks, a mountain rose
abruptly. In the field that separated them from the
mountain behind them, there were a couple of ram-
shackle privies and some clotheslines tied to trees and
a railroad track and a rusted automobile body and a
dirty river called Rockhouse Creek. The leader of the
film crew was a Canadian named Hugh O'Connor.
Widely acclaimed as the co-producer of the Labyrinth
show at Expo 67 in Montreal, O'Connor had been hired
by Francis Thompson, an American filmmaker, to work

· 1 ·

on a film Thompson was producing for the American pavilion at HemisFair in San Antonio. O'Connor went up to three of the shacks and asked the head of each household for permission to take pictures. When each one agreed, O'Connor had him sign the customary release forms and gave him a token payment of ten dollars — a token that, in this case, happened to represent a month's rent. The light was perfect in the valley, and the shooting went well. Theodore Holcomb, the associate producer of the film, was particularly struck by the looks of a miner, still in his work clothes and still covered with coal dust, sitting in a rocking chair on one of the porches. "He was just sitting there scratching his arm in a listless way," Holcomb said later. "He had an expression of total despair. It was an extraordinary shot — so evocative of the despair of that region."

The shot of the coal miner was good enough to be included in the final version of the film, and so was a shot of a half-dozen children who, somehow, lived with their parents in one of the tiny shacks. After about an hour and a half, the crew was ready to leave, but someone had noticed a woman come out of one of the shacks and go to the common well to draw some water, and she was asked to repeat the action for filming. As that last shot was being completed, a woman drove up and told the filmmakers that the man who owned the property was coming to throw them off of it. Then she drove away. A couple of minutes later, another car arrived, and a man — a thin, bald man — leaped out. He was holding a pistol. "Get off my property!" he shouted again and again. Then he shot twice. No one was hit. The filmmakers kept moving their equipment toward their cars across the road while trying to tell the man that they were leaving. One of them said that the man must be shooting blanks. "Get off my property!" he kept screaming. Hugh O'Connor, who was lugging a heavy battery across the highway, turned to say that they were going. The man held the pistol in both hands and pulled the trigger again. "Mr. O'Connor briefly looked down in amazement, and I saw a hole in his chest," Holcomb later testified in court. "He saw it and he looked up in despair and said, 'Why did you have to do that?' and, with blood coming from his mouth, he fell to the ground."

Whitesburg, a town about twelve miles from Jeremiah, is the county seat of Letcher County — headquarters for the county court, the sheriff, and assorted coal companies and anti-poverty agencies. Word that someone had been killed reached Whitesburg quickly, but for a couple of hours there was some confusion about just who the victim was. According to various stories, the dead man had been a representative of the Army Corps of Engineers, a Vista volunteer, or a C.B.S. cameraman — any of whom might qualify as a candidate for shooting in Letcher County. The Corps of Engineers had proposed building the Kingdom Come Dam across Rockhouse Creek, thereby flooding an area that included Jeremiah, and some opponents of the dam had been saying that the first government man who came near their property had better come armed. Throughout Eastern Kentucky, local political organizations and coal-mining interests had warned that community organizers who called themselves Vistas or Appalachian Volunteers or anything else were nothing but another variety of Communists — three of them had been arrested on charges of attempting to overthrow the government of Pike County — and even some of the impoverished people whom the volunteers were supposedly in Kentucky to help viewed them with fear and suspicion. A number of television crews had been to Letcher County to record the despair that Holcomb saw in the face of the miner sitting on the front porch. Whitesburg happens to be the home of Harry M. Caudill, a lawyer who drew attention to the plight of the mountain people in 1963 with an eloquent book called *Night Comes to the Cumberlands*. Television crews and reporters on a tour of Appalachia are tempted to start with Letcher County in order to get the benefit of Caudill's counsel, which is ordinarily expressed in a tone of sustained rage — rage at the profit ratio of out-of-state companies that take the region's natural resources while paying virtually no taxes, rage at the strip mines that are gouged across the mountains and at the mud slides and floods and pollution and ugliness they cause, rage at the local merchants and politicians who make a good living from the trade of welfare recipients or the retainers of coal companies and insist that there is nothing wrong with the economy, and, most of all, rage at the country that could permit it all to happen. "Look what man hath wrought on *that* purple mountain's majesty," he will say as he points out the coal waste on the side of a mountain that had once been beautiful. "A country that treats its land and people this way deserves to perish from the earth."

In the view of Caudill and of Tom Gish, the liberal editor of the *Mountain Eagle,* a Letcher County weekly, the reactions of people in Jeremiah to the presence of O'Connor's film crew — coöperation by the poor people being photographed in their squalid shacks, rage by the man who owned the shacks — were characteristic of Letcher County: a lot of people who are still in Eastern Kentucky after years of welfare or subsistence employment have lost the will to treat their situation as an embarrassment, but outside journalists are particularly resented by the people who have managed to make a living — running a country store or a filling station or a small truck mine, working for the county administration, managing some rental property. They resent the impression that everyone in Eastern Kentucky is like the people who are desperately poor — people whose condition they tend to blame on "just sorriness, mostly." In Letcher County, fear of outsiders by people who are guarding reputations or economic interests blends easily into a deep-rooted suspicion of outsiders by all Eastern Kentucky mountain people, who have always had a fierce instinct to protect their property and a distrust of strangers that has often proved to have been justified. All of the people in Letcher County — people who live in the shacks up remote hollows or people who run stores on Main

Street in Whitesburg — consider themselves mountain people, and, despite an accurate story in the *Mountain Eagle,* many of them instinctively believed that the mountaineer who killed Hugh O'Connor was protecting his property from smart-aleck outsiders who wouldn't leave when they were told.

The mountaineer's name was Hobart Ison. There have always been Isons in Letcher County, and many of them have managed somewhat better than their neighbors. Hobart Ison had inherited a rather large piece of land in Jeremiah — he raised chickens and rented out shacks he himself had built and at one time ran a small sawmill — but he was known mainly as an eccentric, mean-tempered old man. Everyone in Letcher County knew that Hobart Ison had once built and furnished a house for his future bride and — having been rejected or having been afraid to ask or having had no particular future bride in mind — had let the house remain as it was for thirty years, the grass growing up around it and the furniture still in the packing crates. He had occasionally painted large signs attacking the people he thought had wronged him. He was easily enraged by people hunting on his property, and he despised all of the local Democrats, whom he blamed for injustices that included dismissing him from a post-office job. A psychiatrist who examined him after the shooting said, "Any reference to 'game warden' or 'Democrat' will provoke him tremendously." Once, when some local youths were taunting him, he took a shot at them, hitting one in the shoulder. "A lot of people around here would have welcomed them,"

Caudill said of the filmmakers. "They just happened to pick the wrong place."

Streams of people came to visit Ison in the Letcher County jail before he was released on bail. Women from around Jeremiah baked him cakes. When his trial came up, it proved impossible to find a jury. The Letcher County commonwealth's attorney and Caudill, who had been retained by Francis Thompson, Inc., secured a change of venue. They argued that Ison's family relationship in Letcher County was "so extensive as to comprise a large segment of the population," and, through an affidavit signed by three citizens in position to know public opinion, they stated that "the overwhelming expression of sentiment has been to the effect that the defendant did right in the slaying of Hugh O'Connor and that he ought to be acquitted of the offense of murder."

Harlan County is a mountain or two away from Letcher County. In the town of Harlan, benches advertising Bunny Enriched Bread stand outside the front door of the county courthouse, flanking the First World War monument and the Revolutionary War monument and the plaque recalling how many Kentucky courthouses were burned down by each side during the Civil War. On the ground floor of the courthouse, the men who habitually gather on the plain wooden benches to pass the time use old No. 5 cans for ashtrays or spittoons and a large container that once held Oscar Mayer's Pure Lard as a wastebasket. In the courtroom, a plain room with all of its furnishings painted black, the only decoration other than pictures of the men who have served as circuit judge is a framed poster in praise of the country lawyer — and also in praise, it turns out upon close reading, of the Dun & Bradstreet Corporation. The front door of the courthouse is almost always plastered with election stickers. In the vestibule just inside, an old man sits on the floor behind a display of old pocketknives and watchbands and billfolds and eyeglass cases offered for sale or trade.

The commonwealth's attorney of Harlan County is Daniel Boone Smith. Eight or nine years ago, Smith got curious about how many people he had prosecuted or defended for murder, and counted up seven hundred and fifty. He was able to amass that total partly because of longevity (except for a few years in the service during the Second World War, he has been commonwealth's attorney continuously since 1933), partly because he has worked in an area that gives anyone interested in trying murder cases plenty of opportunity (the wars between the unions and the coal operators in Harlan County during the thirties were almost as bloody as the mountain feuds earlier in the century), and partly because he happens to be a quick worker ("Some people will take three days to try a murder case," he has said. "I usually get my case on in a day"). During his first week as commonwealth's attorney of Harlan and an adjoining county, Smith tried five murder cases. These days, Harlan County may have about that many a year, but it remains a violent place. The murders that do occur in mountain counties like Harlan and

Letcher often seem to occur while someone is in a drunken rage, and often among members of the same family — a father shooting a son over something trivial, one member of a family mowing down another who is breaking down the door trying to get at a third. "We got people in this county today who would kill you as quick as look at you," Smith has said. "But most of 'em are the type that don't bother you if you leave them alone." Smith is known throughout Eastern Kentucky for his ability to select jurors — to remember which prospective juror's uncle may have had a boundary dispute with which witness's grandfather twenty years ago — and for his ability to sum up the case for them in their own language once the evidence has been heard. He is an informal, colloquial, storytelling man who happens to be a graduate of the Harvard Law School.

A lack of fervor about convicting Hobart Ison was assumed in Harlan County when he came up for trial there in May 1968. "Before the case, people were coming up and saying, 'He *should've* killed the son of a bitch,'" Smith said later. "People would say, 'They oughtn't to make fun of mountain people. They've made enough fun of mountain people. Let me on the jury, Boone, and I'll turn him loose.'" Smith saw his task as persuading the citizens and the jurors that the case was not what it appeared to be — that the filmmakers were not "a bunch of privateers and pirates" but respectable people who had been commissioned by the United States government, that the film was not another study of how poor and ignorant people were in Eastern Kentucky but a film about the whole United States in which the shots of Eastern Kentucky would take up only a few seconds, that the filmmakers had behaved properly and politely to those they were photographing. "Why, if they had been smart alecks come to hold us up to ridicule, I'd be the last man to try him," Smith assured everyone. It took Smith only a day or so to present his case against Hobart Ison, although it took three days to pick the jury. On the witness stand, the surviving filmmakers managed to avoid admitting to Ison's lawyers that it was the appalling poverty of his tenants that had interested them; they talked about being attracted by expressive family groups and by the convenience of not having to move their equipment far from the road. The defense asked if they were planning to take pictures of the Bluegrass as well as Appalachia. Were they going to make a lot of money from the film? How many millions of viewers would see the pictures of poor Eastern Kentucky people? Had they refused to move? Had they taunted Ison by saying he was shooting blanks? Did the people who signed the release forms really know what they were signing? (At least one of the signers was, like one out of four of his neighbors, unable to read.)

Except for the underlying issue of Eastern Kentucky v. Outsiders, the only issue seriously in contention was Ison's sanity. The director of a nearby mental-health clinic, testifying for the defense, said that Ison was a paranoid schizophrenic. He told of Ison showing up for one interview with long socks worn on the outside of his trouser legs and of his altercations with his neighbors and of his lack of remorse. The prosecution's psychiatrist — an impressive woman from the University of Kentucky who had been retained by Francis Thompson, Inc. — said that Ison had grown up at a time when it was common practice to run people off of property with a gun, and, because he had lived with aging parents or alone ever since childhood, he still followed that practice. Some of Ison's ideas did have "paranoid coloring," she said, but that could be traced to his being a mountaineer, since people in isolated mountain pockets normally had a suspicion of strangers and even of each other. "Socio-cultural circumstances," she concluded, "lead to the diagnosis of an individual who is normal for his culture, the shooting and the paranoid color both being present in other individuals in this culture who are considered normal." In the trial and in the insanity hearing that had earlier found Ison competent to stand trial, Smith insisted that Ison was merely peculiar, not crazy. "I said, 'Now, I happen to like mayonnaise on my beans. Does that make *me* crazy?'" Smith later recalled. "I turned to one of the jurors, a man named Mahan Fields, and I said, 'Mahan, you remember Uncle Bob Woolford, who used to work up at Evarts? Did you ever see Uncle Bob in the winter when he didn't have his socks pulled up over his pants legs to keep out the cold? Now, was Uncle Bob crazy? Why, Mahan, I bet on many a winter morning *you* wore *your* socks over your pants legs.'"

In his summation, Smith saved his harshest words

not for the defendant but for the person who was responsible for bringing Hobart Ison, a mountaineer who
was not quite typical of mountaineers, and Hugh
O'Connor, a stranger with a camera who was not quite
typical of strangers with cameras, into violent conflict.
Judy Breeding — the operator of a small furniture
store near Ison's shacks, and the wife of Ison's cousin
— had testified that she was not only the woman who
told the film crew that Ison was coming but also the
woman who had told Ison that the film crew was on
his property. "Hobart," she recalled saying, "there is
some men over there taking pictures of your houses,
with out-of-state license." Smith looked out toward the
courtroom spectators and suddenly pointed his finger
at Judy Breeding. He told her that he would like to be
prosecuting her, that if it hadn't been for her mouth
Hugh O'Connor would not be in his grave and Hobart
Ison would be back home where he belonged. Later,
Smith caught a glimpse of Mrs. Breeding in the hall,
and he thought he saw her shake her fist at him, smiling. "You know," he said, "I believe the idea that she
had anything to do with bringing that about had never
occurred to her till I mentioned it."

The jury was eleven to one for conviction, but the
one held out. Some people were surprised that Ison
had come that close to being convicted, although it
was generally agreed that the prosecution's psychiatrist
had out-talked the psychiatrist who testified for the
defense. Smith believed that his case had been greatly
strengthened by the fact that the filmmakers had been
respectful, soft-spoken witnesses — not at all smart-

alecky. "If there was anything bigheaded about them," he said, "it didn't show."

The retrial was postponed once, and then was stopped suddenly during jury selection when Smith became ill. On March 24th, Hobart Ison came to trial again. The filmmakers, who had been dreading another trip to Kentucky, were at the county courthouse in Harlan at nine in the morning, ready to repeat their testimony. Although Smith had anticipated even more trouble finding a jury, he was prepared to go to trial. But Ison's lawyers indicated to Smith and Caudill that their client, now seventy, would be willing to plead guilty to voluntary manslaughter, and they finally met Smith's insistence on a ten-year sentence. Ison — wearing a baggy brown suit, his face pinched and red — appeared only briefly before the judge to plead guilty. A couple of hours after everyone arrived, Caudill was on his way back to Whitesburg, where he was working on the case of a Vietnam veteran accused of killing two men during an argument in the street, and the filmmakers were driving to Knoxville to catch the first plane to New York.

The following day, the clerk of the court, a strong-looking woman with a strong Kentucky accent, happened to get into a discussion about the filmmakers with another citizen who had come to know them in the year and a half since Hugh O'Connor's death — a woman with a softer accent and a less certain tone to her voice.

"You know, I asked those men yesterday morning

if they were happy with the outcome," the clerk said. "And they said, 'Yes.' And I said, 'Well, you know, us hillbillies is a queer breed. We are. I'm not offering any apologies when I say that. Us hillbillies *are* a queer breed, and I'm just as proud as punch to be one.'"

"Not all of us are like that," the other woman said. "Mean like that."

"Well, I wouldn't say that man is mean," the clerk said. "I don't guess he ever harmed anybody in his life. They were very nice people. I think it was strictly a case of misunderstanding. I think that the old man thought they were laughing and making fun of him, and it was more than he could take. I know this: a person isolated in these hills, they often grow old and eccentric, which I think they have a right to do."

"But he didn't have a right to kill," the other woman said.

"Well, no," the clerk said. "But us hillbillies, we don't bother nobody. We go out of our way to help people. But we don't want nobody pushin' us around. Now, that's the code of the hills. And he felt like — that old man felt like — he was being pushed around. You know, it's like I told those men: 'I wouldn't have gone on that old man's land to pick me a mess of wild greens without I'd asked him.' They said, 'We didn't know all this.' I said, 'I bet you know it now. I bet you know it now.'"

I've Always Been Clean

West Chester, Pennsylvania
June 1970

JOHN MERVIN, a menacing-looking young man with
long unkempt hair and a shaggy beard, was arrested
for murder last November, confirming the suspicions
of a lot of West Chester citizens about the kind of
crimes young people who looked like that were capable
of perpetrating. The killing that Mervin was accused
of — shooting to death an unemployed nineteen-year-
old named Jonathan Henry — had taken place during
what a newspaper account referred to as a "liquor and
drug party." Anybody who had seen Mervin around
town knew that he wore not only a beard but the jacket
of an outlaw motorcycle gang called the Warlocks.
The lead story on his arraignment in the *West Chester
Daily Local News* revealed that at the time of the killing Mervin was out on bail on a charge of assault with
intent to kill — a charge resulting from an October
shooting in front of a West Chester saloon. The paper
identified Mervin as a student at West Chester State
College, which might be considered an odd thing for a

Warlock to be, except that some people in West Chester were ready to believe almost anything about the kids at West Chester State. The type of school that used to be known as a teachers' college, West Chester State is sufficiently conservative so that someone with a beard would not have been permitted to take classes there a few years ago, but lately the townspeople have been concerned about what they often call "that small element" in the college, an element associated with drugs and demonstrations and bizarre appearance and a lack of respect for accepted values. The small element at West Chester State that worries the townspeople blends easily with a small element among their own children — the most visible result being a band of students or ex-students or drifters occupying the ledges around the steps of the county courthouse, flaunting mustaches and long hair and dirty T-shirts, staring arrogantly at the respectable citizens who walk by.

West Chester has about fifteen thousand citizens, almost all of whom consider themselves respectable. Some of them commute to Philadelphia or to Wilmington or to industries in towns in surrounding Chester County, but West Chester is too self-contained to be considered a suburb. It has a few small industries of its own, plus the legal and bureaucratic machinery that goes with being a county seat. The area that surrounds it still looks rural; the fields and barns of Chadds Ford, familiar from the paintings of Andrew Wyeth, are only a few miles to the south. The law offices clustered around the county courthouse are not in modern office buildings but in brick row houses, marked with neat white shingles. There has always been a lot of talk about history in Chester County — about when the county was founded and how many covered bridges it has and how many generations it has been Republican. But in the last year or two there has also been a lot of talk about drugs and disturbance and crime. The borough council made an effort to improve the police force, buying some new equipment and hiring the chief of county detectives, Thomas Frame, as police chief, at a considerable raise in pay. But a series in the local paper last June said that marijuana was easily available a few steps from the courthouse, the black people of West Chester continued to raise questions about equal treatment, and the kids on the ledges around the courthouse steps continued to symbolize all that menaced the traditional tranquillity of West Chester. The arrest of John Mervin for shooting Jonathan Henry caused some angry outbursts about just how far things had gone with the "hippies." (Although motorcycle gangs have been known to break up peace demonstrations and harass flower children, West Chester citizens tend to bunch all oddly dressed people together as hippies.) Then, a few days after the arrest, Chief Frame held a press conference to announce that John Mervin was an undercover police officer, having been recruited from the Warlocks and secretly sworn in a couple of months before. The police arrested a dozen or so people, most of them from around the college, for having sold drugs to Mervin. Frame announced that thanks to Mervin's efforts the police force had gained possession of forty-eight thousand dollars' worth of dangerous drugs. Mervin, who appeared at the press conference in a neat business suit, said that the arrests resulting from his work would "nearly annihilate any drug distribution" in West Chester. The chief, without commenting on the details of the shootings, said Mervin had "handled himself in the best manner a police officer could" and would begin to work on regular police shifts. John Mervin became a hero.

After it was revealed that Mervin had been an undercover agent, the *Philadelphia Inquirer* decided that he was not merely a student but an honor student, as well as a former high-school football star — a young man who, underneath that hippie disguise, had precisely the attributes any American parent would be proud of. In an *Inquirer* story headlined " 'HIPPIE POLICEMAN' LIVED IN DEGRADATION AND FEAR," Mervin said that the most difficult part of his assignment was not the physical danger but the frustration of not being able to tell his loved ones that he was actually a policeman. "They thought I had gotten into bad company," he said. They were, of course, right: by his own account, Mervin had been in the Warlocks, a group that takes some pride in being considered just about the worst company in eastern Pennsylvania, for two years before anybody approached him about being a policeman. But the stories in the Philadelphia papers made it sound as if practically anything Mervin had ever done was part of the hippie disguise that he had manfully suffered under until he was at last able to throw it off, the drug traffic in West Chester having finally been annihilated. "His love of his motorcycle gained him admission into the Warlocks motorcycle gang two years ago," the *Inquirer* piece said. "And that helped him in his disguise." In a later piece, the *Philadelphia Bulletin* reported the assurance of Mervin's contact man in the police department that Mervin was "always polite, never using elsewhere words and actions he had to use as a hippie drug purchaser and twilight world character." Mervin told the *Inquirer* that his first action after his identity was revealed was to call his mother.

Although the initial reaction in West Chester to Chief Frame's announcement was overwhelming support of Mervin, the support was not unanimous. The October shooting outside the West Chester saloon had been investigated only perfunctorily by the West Chester police after Mervin was arraigned and released on bail. But the killing of Jonathan Henry had taken place in an apartment behind a restaurant-and-bar just outside West Chester, in the jurisdiction of the West Goshen Township police, who continued their investigation even after Chief Frame publicly expressed his confidence in Mervin's innocence. The district attorney's office made it clear that it was pursuing the murder charge, and eventually it even got a preliminary hearing held on the October shooting — a hearing that produced the testimony of a couple of witnesses that

Mervin, after an argument at the bar, had shot his victim in the leg and then had stood over him and shot him in the back. Chief Frame hinted that the district attorney was sore at not having been informed in advance of Mervin's mission and that the other law-enforcement agencies in the county resented West Chester's success in arresting drug dealers. Frame supported Mervin's story that the October shooting had been in self-defense; after the man who had been shot in the back testified, the West Chester police arrested him, on a complaint by Officer Mervin.

Some people familiar with the drug scene in West Chester scoffed at the notion that arresting some college kids for offenses such as selling Mervin a Chiclets box full of LSD tablets had had any effect on the drug traffic. The college crowd began to tell anyone who would listen that Mervin, far from being an honor student, had for a couple of years been a motorcycle tough who bragged about his violence — a bully who had merely redirected his bullying toward coercing people into selling him drugs. Some conversations among West Chester citizens were not about Mervin's heroism but about why someone with his background was sworn in as a policeman and why he was allowed to continue after the first shooting and why he was getting such vigorous support from the police department. "I would like to know what line of duty Mervin was performing on both October 4 and November 19," someone eventually wrote to the *Daily Local News*. "Or who has something on whom?"

Black people in West Chester have the wariness that black people anywhere would have toward a policeman who shoots two people within six weeks, and they have even more reason than most black people to be worried about having an armed former member of a motorcycle gang patrolling the town in a police car. Last Labor Day, during a demonstration in the Chester County town of Parkesburg, a prominent black leader named Harry Dickinson was shot to death, and three members of a motorcycle gang called the Pagans were among those accused (but not convicted) of his murder. No Warlocks had been named by Mervin as drug dealers; when the preliminary hearing on the October shooting was finally held, there were complaints that witnesses testifying against Mervin were intimidated not only by threats of arrest from the West Chester police but by the threat implied by the presence of six attentive Warlocks in the courtroom. Liberals in West Chester were concerned about what has developed in other parts of the country into a sort of alliance between the police and the motorcycle gangs, with the gangs almost in the role of police auxiliaries in the rougher dealings with peace demonstrators and black people and students. At a West Chester borough-council meeting not long after Chief Frame's press conference, the only black councilman moved that, in line with the procedure followed elsewhere when a policeman is accused of a felony, Mervin be suspended until he was exonerated. The motion failed to get a second.

Mervin continued to ride in a police car, carrying

a gun, and he began to appear with Chief Frame around the county to lecture on the evils of drugs — explaining to service clubs and P.-T.A.s and high-school assemblies that "popping a pill" meant taking a tablet and that "acid" meant LSD. The forty-eight thousand dollars' worth of drugs that Mervin had captured — Frame's estimate of the retail price of the drugs Mervin had purchased for twenty-two hundred dollars in borough funds — became fifty thousand dollars at some point in the lecture series. As time went on, it was quoted occasionally as a hundred and thirty-five thousand dollars. The kids around the courthouse steps began to put on mock drug-buying scenes for the benefit of the passing citizens: "Hey, you got any grass to sell?" "No, but I hear there's a guy down at the police station . . ."

On January 26th, a Chester County grand jury indicted Mervin for the murder of Jonathan Henry. West Chester had a new mayor by then, the first Democratic mayor in a century or so, and on the evening after the grand-jury decision he ruled that Mervin had been a special officer whose duties were at an end. There was angry reaction to both the indictment and the mayor's ruling. A number of policemen staged a brief protest in which they handed in their guns — apparently symbolically, since they took them right back when Chief Frame told them to. The police started a John A. Mervin Defense Fund. A number of letters to the *Daily Local News* said that the borough was behaving shoddily by taking away the gun and the position of a man who had saved untold numbers of the community's children from the perils of drugs and had since reported attempts on his life by the murderous elements who control the drug traffic. The borough council, overriding the mayor, voted to hire, and immediately suspend, Mervin as a regular rather than special police officer — guaranteeing that a salary would be put aside for him while the cases were in court and that West Chester would have, among its other historical claims, the distinction of having hired as a policeman someone under indictment for two felonies, one of them murder. A few days later, Mervin reported that he had been shot in the thigh with a .22 while he lay watching television. The mayor felt compelled to write a letter to the *Daily Local News* stating that the decision to end Mervin's service and take away his gun had been made with the approval of Chief Frame and in the best interests of Mervin as well as of the borough. "The futile debate which councilmen and the mayor engaged in on Wednesday night regarding Mervin's pay fades into insignificance today in light of what occurred last night," the *Daily Local News* editorialized the day after Mervin was shot. "What are a few hundred dollars compared to the life of a man who risked everything in order to smash a flourishing drug ring in West Chester?"

"There are only two opinions in West Chester about Mervin," a local reporter said when Mervin came to trial for murder this month. "Either he's a trigger-happy thug who conned the cops or he's a dedicated police officer." People on both sides thought that public opinion was about evenly divided, the word of mouth against Mervin having partly undercut almost universally laudatory press notices. Some of Mervin's most vocal support was judged to be based on a fear of drugs ("Drugs have become such a fearful thing people want to stop the problem and they don't care how," Devere Ponzo, head of the Chester County Black Action Committee, has said. "If a couple of people get killed — tough"); some of it may have come from political considerations (it was thought that raising questions might have been insulting not only to the chief of police but to the Republican establishment that supported him); some of it was undoubtedly a matter of ideology (one group that backed the John A. Mervin Defense Fund — the Association of Alert Citizens, a group that grew out of an anti-sex-education organization called Taxpayers for Decency — based its support partly on the ground that, in the words of one of its spokesmen, "we support the police — period"). But a lot of the talk about the Mervin case in West Chester emphasizes, aside from any political or ideological or anti-drug feeling, how much people *want* to believe in John Mervin. Some people in Chester County (and in the newsrooms of Philadelphia newspapers) seem to have fastened on the Mervin case as a belated sign that the threatening and inexplicable manifestations of the youth culture are not true after all — that the long-haired arrogant-looking kids around the courthouse steps might also throw off *their* disguises and reveal themselves to be honor students and former high-school football stars and battlers against the deadly menace of drugs, that other mothers who are worried about their children's having fallen in with bad company might be told, as John Mervin's mother was told, that it was all an illusion. As the pool of jurors — most of them middle-aged or elderly people, virtually all of them white — walked into the courthouse on the first day of Mervin's trial, one of the usual "hippies," a thin young man with long hair, sat cross-legged on the ledge next to the courthouse steps. He stared at them with a slight smile, occasionally taking a swig of orange juice out of a quart bottle. When any of the jurors being examined said that he already had a firm opinion about the case, both the assistant district attorney and the defense lawyer assumed the opinion was that John Mervin was innocent.

The John Mervin who appeared at the trial was clean-shaven and dressed in summer-weight Ivy League clothes — a baby-faced, somewhat stout young man who answered his elders with polite "Yes, sir"s and "No, sir"s. It would have taken an extraordinary leap of imagination to envision him as a hoodlum biker, dressed in a greasy Warlock jacket, swinging a chain — except, of course, to the extent that he had to wear a costume in the line of duty. (When Mervin testified that he had joined the Warlocks two and a half years before, his attorney said, "Were you engaged in any *other* activities that made you valuable as a police officer?") Mervin testified that after being recruited by Chief Frame he had let his clothing and hair become unkempt and had started attending psychedelic and exotic parties. Trying to show that Mervin had not had to play any role to be accepted in local low life, the assistant district attorney asked him if it wasn't true that as an undercover man he wore the same clothing he had worn as a private citizen, merely allowing it to get a bit dirtier. Mervin looked offended. "I've always been clean," he said. According to Mervin, Jonathan Henry had been shot as he was about to shoot a West Chester State student named Jeffrey Saltzman, whom Henry suspected of being an undercover policeman — a scene precisely like those conjured up by Chief Frame's statements that as an undercover man Mervin had constantly risked his life in "this drug jungle." Saltzman, who happens to be the son of the mayor of a tough Delaware River town named Marcus Hook and the nephew of a West Chester policeman, appeared as a defense witness to corroborate the story. He turned out to be a husky, collegiately dressed young man who also said "Yes, sir" and "No, sir." When the assistant district attorney, trying to argue that Saltzman had been a prospect for membership in the Warlocks, asked him why he had had one of his ears pierced, people in the courtroom looked flabbergasted — as if someone had, for reasons too bizarre to contemplate, asked Saltzman why he had begun talking to his friends in Urdu or why he had taken up the lute.

The witnesses against Mervin made no claim to being the type of people West Chester parents would be proud of. A West Chester State student testified that he had found Mervin's Warlock jacket in his front yard, and that Mervin, saying that Jonathan Henry had worn the jacket while assaulting a girl, had sworn vengeance. The student had long hair and a mustache; the only question he was asked by the defense attorney was one eliciting the admission that he knew some of the people against whom Mervin had brought charges of dealing in drugs. The fourth person present at the scene of the shooting — Eugene Moran, the tenant of the apartment where the shooting took place — testified that Mervin, with Saltzman's acquiescence, had shot Henry in cold blood; the assistant district attorney argued that the bullet angles supported Moran's story and made the Mervin-Saltzman version physically impossible. But Moran also admitted having told the grand jury that he remembered nothing about the crime; he said he had been threatened by Mervin and Saltzman and was terrified of talking. Moran, a thin man in his thirties who was wearing a suit that seemed too large, had been to college and was said to be fond of discussing philosophy — although on the night in question he happened to be speechless from overconsumption of Southern Comfort and water. He didn't look in the least collegiate.

Jonathan Henry, as described in court, seemed even more disreputable than those who had testified that he might have been murdered. Michael Thompson, a

Warlock who appeared in a kind of Hitler mustache, took the stand to describe how he and Henry spent their days. Henry would come by for him every day about three or four in the afternoon, and then they would "just ride around, get some beer and drink, do anything we wanted to, really." Thompson said they occasionally dealt in LSD, in a minor way, for gas money. The proprietor of a bar frequented by the Warlocks testified that Henry had waved a gun around, threatening people, the night before he died. Mervin testified that Henry had bragged to him about shooting someone — or, as Mervin put it, about having to "dust somebody off."

Henry, in fact, sounded remarkably like the description that West Chester State students offer of John Mervin. But after a week's testimony the assistant district attorney was under no illusions about being able to persuade the jury that John Mervin was anything but a decent young officer who had once been obliged to pretend to be like Jonathan Henry. After reminding the jury that they were not trying "the police or police in general or the issue of Support Your Local Police," the assistant district attorney further reminded them that neither sympathy nor prejudice should affect a jury's decision — and the sympathy and prejudice he was talking about was sympathy for John Mervin, a young college student, and prejudice against Jonathan Henry, a violent drug peddler. The judge repeated the admonition in his charge: "We are not here concerned with whether Henry deserved to live."

It took the jury approximately twenty-five minutes to reach a verdict of not guilty. Afterward, in the corridor, the jurors were having a final chat with each other when Mervin walked by, holding hands with a pretty girl. A number of the jurors walked up to shake his hand and pat him on the back and wish him luck. "Thank you. Thank you, sir," Mervin said to one of them. They smiled at him as he walked on down the corridor — a nice-looking, neatly dressed, polite young man who did look as if he had always been clean.

Jim, Tex, and
the One-armed Man

Center Junction, Iowa
February 1971

JIM BERRY came to Center Junction in 1962 and
didn't do much that anybody approved of from then
until the time he left, rather suddenly, last June. A
native of Nashville, Tennessee, he had ended up in
Center Junction because a decrepit house there happened to become available some time after he married
a woman from a nearby town. He hadn't been in the
house long before he was in an argument with the
town council about whether he could be forced to in-
stall a septic tank. His steadiest source of support for
a houseful of children and stepchildren seemed to be
Aid for Dependent Children payments — a form of
welfare small-town people in Iowa tend to consider a
government subsidy for random breeding. Some people
in Center Junction say they found Jim Berry a likable
person when he was sober, but nobody liked him when
he was drunk. Dorothy's Tap, the only tavern in town,

wouldn't serve him. When Jim Berry drank, one citizen recalls, "he was always a-needlin' and a-pushin'." He owned a shotgun and a rifle and a pistol, and it was said that he could throw a knife well enough to take the bark off a tree. There were stories in Center Junction about people who had called Jim Berry's bluff and faced him down — the way a Western-movie hero might face somebody down in a bar — but a lot of people, aware, perhaps, that they really might not act like a Western-movie hero if Berry started needling them, feared and resented him. Someone who asks a citizen of Center Junction for an explanation of why Jim Berry was so belligerent when drunk is likely to get a simple, direct answer. "He had Indian blood in him," the citizen will say. "Liquor makes 'em wild."

People found it irritating that Berry always seemed to get away with things. Nobody in Center Junction has ever got away with much. Most people who live in Center Junction live there because they were born there. Since there isn't any work to speak of in the town itself — it's a fading little farm town of only about two hundred people — a lot of people drive to work every day in places like Monticello or Anamosa or even Cedar Rapids, thirty miles away. Some of their children get tired of driving and move to Cedar Rapids. Jim Berry never woke up early on a cold morning to drive to the Cuckler Steel Span Company, in Monticello. He was an upholsterer by trade, but he worked at it only sporadically. After an operation on his back a few years ago, he began drawing Social Security disability payments. People in Center Junction muttered that his back seemed all right for hunting or fishing or leaning over a bar. Nothing serious seemed to happen to Berry when the deputy sheriff picked him up for drunkenness or driving without a license. People in Center Junction often say that Jim Berry once killed a child on the highway in the southwestern part of the state. In fact, a manslaughter charge against him was dismissed; he served a few months for leaving the scene of an accident. When people mention the case, they seem angry not only that a child died but also that Berry seemed to have got away with something.

Center Junction people admit that when Berry did do upholstery it was excellent work — work that made it easy to believe him when he said that in Nashville he and his brother did the jobs for the city's top four decorators. In fact, people in Center Junction say that Jim Berry was good at whatever interested him. "There ain't nothing Jim couldn't tell you; there ain't nothing he couldn't fix, or even make," one of them has said. "I don't know what his I.Q. was supposed to be, but something fantastic." A couple of years ago, Berry took a correspondence course in electronics. He fixed a few radios and television sets — and fixed them well — but the main result of the course was that he became an avid Citizen's Band radio operator, installing an elaborate rig in the shed he sometimes used as an upholstery shop. He got to know Citizen's Band slang, so that, wanting to sign off to another CBer and send regards to the man's wife, he could say, "Seventy-threes, good buddy, and a stack of eighty-eights for the XYL." He even went to a couple of CB jamborees. He was particularly proud of having the most powerful station in the area. ("Jim had to be top of the hill," one of the townspeople says.) By "skipping" signals off the ionosphere, CBers often operate at distances much greater than the hundred and fifty miles permitted by F.C.C. regulations, and Berry boasted of being able to talk to West Germany every morning. Because skipping is against the regulations, CBers who do it identify themselves with "skip handles" rather than real names or call letters, and often use the handles even for legal conversations. Berry liked to call himself the Bald-headed Hippie or Freddy the Freeloader for long-distance broadcasting. The skip handle he preferred locally was Buckshot.

Around June of 1969, Jim Berry got into a CB conversation with a man who had an even more powerful station than he did — a man called Tex Yarborough, who lived in Maquoketa, Iowa, about twenty-five miles east. It turned out that Tex Yarborough and Jim Berry had a lot in common — although Tex was only about thirty, a dozen years younger than Jim. Like Jim, Tex had ended up in his wife's home county, having come up from Dallas a couple of years before. He had three rifles and a pistol. Tex was a machinist by trade, but, like Jim, he didn't make a fetish out of steady work. In fact, he didn't work for the year he knew Jim Berry. (When Mrs. Yarborough was asked later how her husband managed, with no income, to support a wife, three children, a roomful of radio equipment, and three cars, each car with its own CB mobile unit, she said, "Credit. We had good credit.") Like Berry, Tex was a proud son of his home state. He ordinarily wore cowboy boots and a cowboy hat, and he apparently claimed at times to be a cousin of Ralph Yarborough, who was then the senior senator from Texas. Tex had been in trouble for offenses like passing bad checks and assault and battery, and he had been in jail in Texas. His skip handles were Short Stuff, Tex, and Dirty Pierre.

Jim Berry and Tex Yarborough became friends. They spent a lot of time talking on the radio — to each other and to people like Lumberjack and Blue Goose and Sparkplug and the Mustanger. That fall, they met often to go hunting or fishing or drinking. They had their differences. Jim believed that Tex sometimes "threw a carrier" on him — that is, keyed his microphone so that people talking on weaker stations would be cut off. (Center Junction people claim that Jim was in the habit of throwing carriers himself.) One night, when Jim and Tex returned to the Yarborough house after visiting a few taverns, they had a scuffle that consisted of — depending on which story is believed — Tex's knocking Jim down for making an offensive remark to Mrs. Yarborough or Jim's trying to help Tex to bed drunk and being attacked for his trouble. But Tex put in some radio equipment for Jim, and Jim, in return, agreed to make some new cushions and a skirt for the Yarboroughs' couch — a project that was only half-finished when a fire in Jim's shed burned up the rest of Tex's material. According to Berry, there was even talk about a partnership: in a building Yarborough knew about in Maquoketa, Jim would do upholstering while Tex acted as salesman and deliverer. That was supposedly the project Jim wanted to talk about when he asked Tex to come by — about a year after they had met — and they went to Lou's Place in Monticello, where they met the one-armed man.

Lou's Place, identified by a Hamm's Beer sign on a side street in Monticello, has a beer-company décor. There is a Schlitz clock, a Miller's clock, and three Hamm's clocks. Calendars are by Budweiser, Pabst, and Hamm's; lamps by Pabst, Hamm's, and Schlitz. About the only objects of non-brewery art are three tapestries — peacocks, mountain goats, and horses — that Lou (Louise Garrett) bought once from a foreign-looking travelling man. In Lou's Place, people often argue in loud voices and men use bad language in front of women, who use bad language back. But the most abusive customer can usually be put out by a barmaid, who may be only five feet two but has the advantage of being sober, of having put out a number of similarly abusive customers in the past, and of holding the power to refuse service indefinitely. Jim and Tex arrived at about noon on a Friday in June — Tex a heavyset man wearing his customary cowboy boots and cowboy hat, Jim a taller, thinner man with a small, tired-looking face. They had come in about the same time the day before, and Bonnie Balsiger, the barmaid on duty, remembered them well — particularly Tex Yarborough. "He told me, 'I don't know how I ended up in a dumpy little town like this,'" she said later. "I told him that no one drug him into the town and if he didn't like it he could get the hell out of it." At one point in that first afternoon, Bonnie, leaning over the bar to pick up a glass, had noticed that Yarborough had a knife in his lap. He was talking about using it to slice up Jim Berry.

"You're going to have to forgive me for what I'm going to have to do," Tex told Bonnie.

"Whatever you're going to do, don't do it in here," she said. She ordered Tex to put away the knife or get out, and he put away the knife. He and Jim had spent the rest of the afternoon drinking together. "He was real picky, real boisterous, real loudmouthed," Bonnie said later of Tex. "The kind you have to cool down."

On Friday afternoon, Tex and Jim spent some time drinking with a group of pipeline workers, including a one-armed man named Jim Leonard. Wet weather had stopped work on a gas line being laid near what Jim Leonard remembered as "some little ole bitty place south of Anamosa." He had come into Lou's Place to ask his boss for an advance on his wages so he could drive home for the weekend to Bald Knob, Arkansas, where he and a number of other pipeliners live between jobs — relying on two subscriptions to a pipeline newsletter from Houston to keep them informed about where the next job might be. He had stayed around for a few hours to drink. Leonard's boss, agreeing to the advance, had laid a hundred-dollar bill on the table. The hundred-dollar bill was just about the conversational high point in a long afternoon at Lou's Place that was otherwise marked by Lou's telling Tex Yarborough that he was being too argumentative to be allowed at the pipeliners' table and by a number of people present getting into an argument about something called a water dog. (Jim Berry said water dogs were very common in Tennessee — "kind of like a lizard but with skin like a catfish" — and made excellent bait for striped bass. The other side questioned not only whether a water dog made good bait for striped bass but whether there *was* such a thing as a water dog. For Lou's Place, the argument was, as Jim Berry later described it, "a regular argument — a group argument.") At one point in the afternoon, Berry had asked Jim Leonard, the one-armed man, for a ride home — Center Junction being, in a manner of speaking, on the way to Bald Knob — and at about seven they left for Berry's house, stopping on the way so that Berry could buy a pint of Jim Beam.

At Center Junction, Berry showed Leonard his radio set and his guns, and then they sat down for a drink in the living room — a room with a floor of worn linoleum and walls decorated with a three-dimensional picture of the Statue of Liberty and an operating cuckoo clock and a picture of a saucer-eyed soldier over a passage about mother love ("A mother's love is like a rose hung on your chest . . ."). Mrs. Berry was not living with her husband at the time — she and the children were in an apartment in Anamosa, the county seat — and Berry made a phone call to Maquoketa trying, fruitlessly, to find a couple of girls. Not long after that, Tex Yarborough came in the door. "I want that hundred-dollar bill," he said to Jim Leonard. There was a brief scuffle, and then Leonard ran out to the front yard, only to be caught by Yarborough and knocked to the ground. Suddenly the one-armed man kicked at Yarborough and jumped to his feet. "They're trying to kill me!" he shouted. "They're trying to rob me!" And, with a terrified look on his face, he ran down the street — at a speed he later estimated at five hundred miles an hour. Tex slowly walked back up to the house, where Jim Berry was standing in the doorway, holding his 20-gauge shotgun. Tex was only a couple of feet from the door when Jim fired the gun. Tex seemed to stand still for a moment. Then he turned and walked off the porch into the yard. "You shot me, you rat," he said. "You shot me." He walked across the street and sat down next to an old stump. Then he got up and walked back across the street and crawled into the front seat of the one-armed man's car. He was there when the ambulance arrived. The deputy sheriff came and took Jim Berry to jail in Anamosa. One of the neighbors locked Tex Yarborough's car. The motor was still running, and so was the Citizen's Band mobile unit.

Tex Yarborough died later that evening, from the damage done by a shotgun wound in the stomach.

When Jim Berry came to trial in Anamosa last fall, he said that he had shot Tex in self-defense — that Tex had been holding what seemed like a knife when he stood over the one-armed man, that Tex had muttered, "You're next, Berry, you son of a bitch," as he slowly approached the door, that Tex had reached for the gun. The way the events were seen by some people who live in a neat white house across the street — people who wouldn't have been surprised at just about anything they saw going on in Jim Berry's ragged front yard — Yarborough stepped onto the porch, the screen door flew open, and he was shot. Jim Leonard — referred to by everybody involved as "the one-armed man" — said that he, too, had seen something that he thought was a knife in Yarborough's hand, and that Yarborough had said, "Give me that money or I'll cut your goddam throat." The prosecution pointed out that Berry had said nothing about a knife until a few hours after he was in custody — at which point the deputy sheriff had returned to look around the yard, finding only a cowboy hat. The jury failed to reach a verdict.

A lot of people in Center Junction were outraged that Jim Berry had apparently got away with something again. As his second trial approached, and the news got out that the county had hired a special prosecutor from Cedar Rapids to help the county attorney, it was said around town that if Berry was found innocent and returned to Center Junction, some of his neighbors would sell their houses and leave. The second trial was held in Cedar Rapids, so not many

Center Junction people could attend regularly, but a number of them showed up for the closing arguments — the men identifiable by the start of beards being grown for this summer's Center Junction centennial celebration. Berry's mother came up from Tennessee for the trial. (In answer to a reporter's question, she said that Jim's grandmother on his father's side had been part Indian; she volunteered the information that Jim, as a fourteen-year-old who had managed to join the Navy during the war, had had his picture in papers all over the country for collecting so many dimes for the campaign against polio.) The evidence was much the same as it had been at the first trial. Berry again testified that Tex had told him about past acts of violence — about pulling a man off a barstool at the Wagon Wheel in Maquoketa and stomping his face in, about beating a man's brains out with a frying pan. The jury, after two days of deliberations, failed to reach a verdict. The jurors had seemed attentive but puzzled. Why didn't Berry just lock the door if he had been threatened? But why would he shoot Tex Yarborough if he hadn't been threatened? But then why would people spend a weekday afternoon at Lou's Place arguing about water dogs?

Sergei Kourdakov

Southern California
May 1973

ON NEW YEAR'S EVE, not long after midnight, the sheriff's department of San Bernardino County sent a patrol car to Running Springs in response to the telephone call of a young woman who said that her boyfriend had shot himself. Running Springs is a tiny town in the mountains, at the point where the road up from San Bernardino splits into one highway going toward Lake Arrowhead and another toward the ski resort at Big Bear. It has an oddly temporary look, as if it had been put up absentmindedly and might some-day be dismantled in the same way. The attempts at the ersatz-chalet style that sometimes distinguish mountain resorts from supermarkets in southern California seem halfhearted — a piece of artificial timbering here, a few loops cut out of a knotty-pine porch railing there. Running Springs has a couple of motels that catch some overflow from the resorts on a busy weekend, but they look less like modern California motels than like what used to be called tourist cabins.

When the sheriff's officers arrived, a distraught young woman led them to a room at the Giant Oaks Motel. A muscular young man dressed in a T-shirt and blue jeans lay on the floor between the two beds. A champagne bottle and a glass were at his feet. There was a bottle of strawberry wine on the television set. On the desk, there was a typewriter with a partly typed page in it. A .38-calibre Smith & Wesson revolver lay on the rug. The young man had been killed by a gunshot in the head. The following day, the *Los Angeles Herald-Examiner* ran a front-page banner headline that said, "RUSS DEFECTOR DEATH UNDER PROBE."

In some circles, Sergei Kourdakov had been known not just as a Russ Defector but as a repentant, evangelical, born-again Christian Russ Defector. Since last summer, he had been travelling to churches around the country as a speaker for Underground Evangelism, a Glendale organization that describes itself as "a ministry to the suffering church in the Communist World." The issue of Underground Evangelism's monthly magazine that had just been published carried a chapter of Kourdakov's reminiscences and an advertisement for a cassette tape, available for a donation of four dollars, of the Sergei Kourdakov story — "A Persecutor of Christians Now Witnessing for Christ." The cassette, a recording of one of Kourdakov's public appearances, has an introduction in which L. Joe Bass, the founder and president of Underground Evangelism, offers a dramatic account of Sergei Kourdakov's first twenty-one years — his triumphs as a model young Communist and Soviet naval cadet, his awful adventures as the leader of a brutal attack group that raided one hundred and fifty underground churches in the region of Kamchatka, his decision to leap from a Russian trawler off the west coast of Canada, his miraculous swim through icy waters to shore, his conversion, his amazement at discovering that a Russian-language Bible presented to him by a Canadian pastor was identical to the Bibles confiscated from the Christians he had once beaten and despised, his joy at finding in Underground Evangelism the very organization whose smuggling efforts had provided those Bibles to the persecuted Christians of Kamchatka. Underground Evangelism had featured refugee Eastern European Christians before but never one who was a repentant persecutor of Christians as well. Orders were already coming in for his forthcoming autobiography.

Underground Evangelism was accustomed to reporting the death of Christians at the hands of Communist torturers; that had become, in fact, something of a specialty. The death of a Christian — Underground Evangelism's featured Christian — by his own hand while he was sharing a motel room with a seventeen-year-old girl was another matter. Within a week of the shooting, Underground Evangelism had issued a press release stating that suicide, which had been mentioned in some early press reports, was out of the question, and that the circumstances of Kourdakov's death remained "strange" and "uncertain." His life had been threatened several times by Russian-speaking men, the release said, and he had once told Bass, "If you ever hear I have had an accident or committed suicide, don't believe it. I know how the Soviet police work, because I was one of them." The problems Underground Evangelism could expect from the press became obvious immediately after the shooting when an item appeared in Toronto, where Kourdakov had lived before coming to the United States. The *Toronto Star* quoted Kourdakov's Toronto pastor as saying that Kourdakov might have succumbed to the fast pace of the American evangelism circuit — part of the fast pace being, in the pastor's view, that Underground Evangelism had been using Kourdakov and exaggerating his career and exposing him to too much publicity. A young woman who said she had known Kourdakov at George Brown College, in Toronto, was quoted as saying that, according to a letter she had received from him, Kourdakov had regretted going into evangelical work and had confessed that he did not, in fact, happen to believe in God.

The San Bernardino coroner's office had pretty much concluded that Kourdakov had killed himself accidentally while playing with the revolver, but Bass said that a county like San Bernardino did not have the facilities to deal with such sophisticated matters as the death of a Soviet defector. "What better time than midnight on New Year's Eve, and what better place than that small, tourist-packed resort area for Sergei Kourdakov to have an 'accident'?," a newsletter sent to the Underground Evangelism mailing list said. "It's a rural county, mainly desert and mountains, with a small population and a relatively small law-enforcement staff." It was not a line of reasoning that pleased the law-enforcement authorities of San Bernardino County. "Any time you have a death such as this, where there was a young man in a motel room, a young girl, and a bottle of wine," the coroner, Bill Hill, told the *San Bernardino Sun,* "I guess you could call it 'strange' and 'uncertain.' "

Attacks on Underground Evangelism over its handling of Sergei Kourdakov had begun from sources that could be expected to be even more persistent than offended county authorities or a suspicious secular press — two neighboring Glendale organizations called Jesus to the Communist World, Inc., and Evangelism to Communist Lands. Glendale, a middle-class section of the Los Angeles sprawl, is a center for ministries to the suffering church in the Communist World more or less the way Seventh Avenue is a center for the garment industry — an industry with which the Glendale missionaries seem to share standards of good will toward the competition. Glendale grew as a center for oppressed-church missions as Eastern European refugees who had moved to town to work for Underground Evangelism took acrimonious leave of U.E. and formed their own organizations. Jesus to the Communist World is run by Richard Wurmbrand and his family — Wurmbrand being a Rumanian Lutheran who wrote a book called *Tortured for Christ* and was, for a while, best known in this country for having removed his shirt before members of the Senate Internal Security Subcommittee to illustrate his testimony that the Communists had left him with eighteen scars in their effort to make him forsake the church. Evangelism to Communist Lands is a smaller operation, run by Haralan Popov and his family. Popov is a Bulgarian; his book, written while he was still with U.E., is called *Tortured for His Faith.*

The three Glendale missions have some difference in emphasis — whether to concentrate on smuggling Bibles in by clandestine couriers, for instance, or to float some of them toward Russia or Cuba on appropriate ocean currents — but their literature tends to tell the same kinds of stories about the need for Christian literature and the need to help the families of jailed and tortured Christian martyrs. They tend to use the same terms, and even the same martyrs. One distinguishing feature of the Wurmbrands' discussion of mission work to the suffering church in the Communist World is their contention that L. Joe Bass has never done much of it, at least not enough to justify the two million dollars U.E. collects every year for that purpose — a contention they have made in a thick report that Bass has answered with a counter-report denying all allegations and accusing Richard Wurmbrand of carrying on a vendetta because he was thwarted in an attempt to take over Underground Evangelism. At first, Jesus to the Communist World reacted to Kourdakov's death merely by accusing Underground Evangelism of exposing him to worldly temptations he was not prepared for in its haste to exploit him. Then it began to question parts of the story told about him — whether there actually could be one hundred and fifty raidable underground churches in Kamchatka, for instance — and his own sincerity. (According to a letter the Wurmbrands circulated, Kourdakov, after falling to the floor of a temple in Toronto and shouting that he was filled with the Holy Spirit, was asked, "With what Ghost are you filled?" and replied, "Money.") Finally, the Jesus to the Communist World literature began saying that Kourdakov not only was not in danger from the K.G.B. but may have been a K.G.B. plant himself. The Popovs, who ordinarily use more restrained language than the Wurmbrands in denouncing Bass, limiting themselves for the most part to charges of lying and deception, said they were saddened that Bass had used Kourdakov instead of giving him the opportunity to grow in Christ. "He was what we call a backslider," Ladin Popov, Haralan's brother, said of Kourdakov recently. "And the wages of sin are death."

Bass explains the defection of people like Wurmbrand and Popov partly as a tendency in "the Eastern European mentality" to prefer small family businesses rather than large, centralized organizations. He says that those who accuse Underground Evangelism of trying to make a martyr out of Sergei Kourdakov are themselves guilty of vilifying the boy in order to further their campaign against Underground Evangelism. According to Bass, such attacks are no more than the leader in the field should expect. "Let's face it," he said recently. "They're interested parties. They're trying to build an organization from the same pool of donors."

At the coroner's inquest, held in San Bernardino the last week in February, the star witness was, of course, the young woman who had been staying with Kourdakov at the Giant Oaks Motel — a blond high-school senior who had met Kourdakov at a church camp. Her parents, also churchgoing people, had invited him to be their houseguest while he was in California. According to the testimony, the parents were aware that Kourdakov and their daughter were going to take a weekend trip together — first to Disneyland and then to the mountains, where they hoped to do some skiing while Sergei worked on the papers he had promised to prepare as part of the effort Senator Strom Thurmond and others in Washington were carrying on to win him permanent residency. A polygraph specialist for the sheriff's office testified that the girl had responded to a question about her sexual relations with Kourdakov at the Giant Oaks — a question that had been included in the polygraph test at her father's insistence — by saying that they "had come close but not completed an act." ("I might say that was the area of the greatest concern of this young lady at the time of the test, as opposed to whether or not she had shot the man," the polygraph expert said. "So I feel we have very definite . . . truthful responses.") As the girl described New Year's weekend in Running Springs, she had spent most of her time watching television while Kourdakov typed away. On New Year's Eve, he had paused to watch the Dick Van Dyke show and some other programs he liked, and then they had shared some champagne, and then, for no apparent reason, he had held the gun up and shot himself.

From what the investigators gathered, Kourdakov may have made a mistake about which way the cylinder turns on a Smith & Wesson .38. The previous day, it was testified, he had taken out one bullet, explaining that he was removing it for safety reasons, and the investigators surmised that he might have thought he was firing an empty chamber. The gun had been borrowed from the girl's father, an electrician, who testified that Kourdakov had his permission to borrow a weapon whenever he felt the need of one. The father had heard that some people in Washington were working on obtaining permission for Kourdakov to carry a gun — ordinarily illegal for an alien — but, he testified, "it's been my sad experience in the past that bureaucracy moves so slow that he would get killed just about the time they got papers on him."

"How many weapons do you own?" the coroner asked.

"Seven," he replied.

Bass offered depositions from churchmen in Washington attesting to what an exuberant, life-loving Christian Kourdakov had been. Some friends of the girl's parents who had met Kourdakov just before the young couple went off for the weekend testified that he had been in fine spirits, and had been particularly delighted with some new custom-fitted ski boots. According to his contract with Underground Evangelism, offered in evidence, Kourdakov had no financial worries. He was receiving a salary of two hundred dollars a week, plus ten per cent of the offerings collected at his speaking engagements (after expenses were deducted) and twenty-five per cent of the cassette take — an arrangement that had permitted him to clear $1,688.01 for the month of October. ("He's done quite well for being a resident of our country for a short period of time," one member of the coroner's jury remarked to the court.) The future looked even brighter, since Kourdakov's contract called for him to receive fifty per cent of the profits from his autobiography. He appeared to have both business and literary plans for the future. The page of typing in his typewriter was not documentation for Senator Thurmond but what appeared to be part of a short story.

Denying charges that Underground Evangelism had exploited Kourdakov, Bass said that the money spent on "developing Mr. Kourdakov into a well-rounded resident far exceeded any remuneration which our organization received as a result of his activities" — or, as the assistant treasurer of U.E. later put it to a reporter, "If you want to look on the cold, hard financial facts, we lost money on the kid." Bass said that Underground Evangelism had been mainly concerned about Kourdakov's "developing and growing into the American way of life." Much of the testimony, of course, indicated that Kourdakov had already grown into the American way of life at the time of his death: a weekend at Disneyland and at a motel, a seventeen-year-old girl more emphatic about her reputation than about murder, strawberry wine, a pair of custom-fitted ski boots, a Thunderbird in the parking lot. Where else but in America, after all, could Kourdakov find, to his ultimate misfortune, that the father of a girl he met at a church camp owned seven weapons?

After three days of testimony, the coroner's jury reached a verdict of accidental death. Bass, under questioning from the coroner, said he was satisfied with the standards of San Bernardino County police work after all. But Underground Evangelism still answers questions about the case by saying that "quiet inquiries" are being made; the last two issues of Underground Evangelism's monthly, both of them devoted almost entirely to Sergei Kourdakov, mention nothing about his gunshot being self-inflicted but talk about his insistence on continuing his work despite the danger. The inquest had, of course, brought out some information embarrassing to Underground Evangelism. The Wurmbrands ordered a copy of the transcript, and Congressman Earl Landgrebe, of Indiana — one of the sponsors of Kourdakov's visa, and a man whose own commitment to the cause is strong enough to have resulted in his being detained in Russia last year for handing out Bibles — said he believed he himself had been exploited by Underground Evangelism. Bass has said that the rank and file of Underground Evangelism supporters remained loyal despite the circumstances of Kourdakov's death — which may indicate that evangelical Christians are more broad-minded than they are usually given credit for or that Underground Evangelism supporters depended for their information on U.E. literature, which gave them nothing to be broad-minded about, having mentioned alcohol not at all and sex only to say, in an early newsletter, that, contrary to rumors, "official sources completely rule out any misconduct in relation to a girl."

The April issue of Underground Evangelism's magazine announced "a fitting memorial to Sergei" — the Sergei Kourdakov Memorial Fund. Kourdakov's book is almost ready. Bass has just returned from a European trip on which he closed a deal for the German rights and began negotiation for publication in England. There have been reports that Kourdakov may have left heirs — some brothers in Russia — but they would probably have difficulty claiming his fifty per cent of the book royalties even if they made their way to Glendale. Clause 11 of his agreement with Underground Evangelism said that he would not "commit any act that will reasonably tend to degrade him or to bring him or U.E. into public contempt, ridicule, or would tend to shock or offend the constituency of U.E. or the Christian church in general." Sergei Kourdakov had obviously broken his contract.

You Always Turn Your Head

Gallup, New Mexico
May 1973

PETE DERIZOTIS, CITY ALCOHOLISM COORDINATOR: *I was in the mayor's office. . . . Somebody knocked. . . . I opened the door. It was Larry Casuse and another Indian fellow.* — Radio Station KGAK live coverage, from the street in front of Stearn's Sporting Goods store, March 1st.

In Gallup, it was taken for granted that employees of the city government would recognize Larry Casuse on sight. A couple of years before, he had been just another one of the Navajo students at Gallup High School — a bright, husky, energetic boy who served as an aggressive linebacker on the football team and as an officer of the Indian Club. Unlike a lot of students who had grown up on or near the huge Navajo reservation that Gallup serves as a trading center, he had brought little firsthand knowledge to the Indian Club's study of Indian ceremonial costumes and Indian dances. In a city where radio advertisements for pickup

trucks are in Navajo, he spoke only English; among
students whose brothers returning from Vietnam were
likely to have felt the need for an Enemy Way cere-
mony, he was accustomed to only Roman Catholic
rituals. His father, a Navajo from the reservation town
of Mexican Springs, had married an Austrian woman
while serving in the Army and had then settled near
Silver City, New Mexico, far from the reservation,
where he found work in the copper mines, and raised
his children among non-Indians. In high school, Larry
had spent a lot of time on Indian Club work — making
costumes, helping to organize the first Gallup High
School powwow — and when he went to the University
of New Mexico, in the fall of 1971, he joined the Kiva
Club, an Indian cultural and social organization that
had been best known for its sponsorship of an annual
dance. When he became president of the Kiva Club
last fall, its interests began to turn from dances to
such questions as whether the university's history text-
books presented a true version of Indian history and
whether the advertisement of a local merchant was
insulting to Indians. By that time, he had also been
active for several months in Indians Against Exploitation, a group of young Navajos in Gallup who had organized to protest against the Gallup Inter-Tribal
Indian Ceremonial on the ground that it was a white-
run business operation that made money for whites
by presenting Indian religion in a cheapened form for
the entertainment of tourists. I.A.E. had expanded its
criticisms to include the way Gallup treated the In-

dians who came in to trade and the Indians who came
in to drink, and Larry Casuse had been to City Hall
before to complain or demand or condemn. When the
State Commission on the Bicentennial Celebration met
in Gallup in January, Casuse had been one of the young
Indians who appeared to say that money should be
spent not for celebrations but for people in need. When
Pete Derizotis opened the door of the mayor's office on
March 1st, the Larry Casuse he recognized had the
look of an Indian militant — blue jeans, long black
hair, a red bandanna worn as a headband.

DERIZOTIS: *They say they want to see the mayor. I say
they will have to wait — he's in a meeting at this time. So
the mayor hollered, "No, let 'em come in. Let 'em come
in." So I let 'em come in. So Casuse pulled his gun right
away. . . .*

A lot of people who knew Larry Casuse were astounded to hear that he had pulled a gun on anyone.
Young Navajos of the type active in I.A.E. have ordinarily gone in for peaceful, even dignified, protest. At
the Gallup Ceremonial in August of 1971, when it was
clear that the most effective tactics would have been
to create enough raucous harassment to frighten away
the tourists, the I.A.E. was interested only in a silent,
almost funereal march. As far as anyone knew, Larry
Casuse had not even been familiar with guns.

There were varying speculations as to what might
have caused him suddenly to take up arms. Some sym-

pathetic whites believed that he might have, in the words of one of them, flipped out. Even as a high-school student, he was the kind of boy sometimes described as "high-strung," and to some people he had appeared increasingly tense at various public appearances in the previous months. Everyone agreed that he had been particularly upset by an accident in which, while driving toward Gallup at three or four in the morning, he struck and killed a young Navajo woman who had apparently wandered onto the highway. He had been tried twice on a charge of not rendering proper assistance — the prosecution and Casuse differed basically on whether, just before his car became mired on a side road and he pounded on the door of a state policeman's house, he had been searching for help or trying to dispose of the body — and a hung jury on the second trial stood eleven to one for conviction. A date for a third trial had just been set. Casuse's remorse about the accident was such that he could not speak of it without weeping. But he believed that the criminal charge was a matter of the authorities' punishing him for his political beliefs, and those who shared the beliefs tended to agree.

In the view of a lot of his Navajo friends, Casuse decided to do something as drastic as abducting the mayor not out of insanity but merely out of impatience and frustration. A lot of people who knew him at the university describe him as someone who "couldn't sit still." He was apparently becoming more and more impatient with the lack of effect the efforts of the young

Indians seemed to have. He was frustrated, his friends say, about his inability to focus attention on conditions in Gallup. In the opinion of one young Navajo who knew him at the university, "He thought he would have to utilize the white man's way of doing things to get anything done — just to shake people up enough to get a few lines in the paper, to grab people in mid-air and say 'Wait a minute! Listen to me!' "

REPORTER: *How did the activity change places over here to the sporting-goods store?*
DERIZOTIS: *With a gun right to the head, he escorted the mayor all the way down. They broke the glass door, and they entered.*

Casuse said nothing that would have made it clear what he intended to do with the mayor. One of his friends from I.A.E. thinks Casuse obviously intended to hold the mayor hostage as a way of negotiating for an investigation into Gallup's treatment of Indians or a compromise on specific demands. Precisely that type of negotiation was taking place at the time at Wounded Knee. When students at the Kiva Club are asked what Casuse might have been up to, they tend to base their answer on a remark he apparently made to the mayor at some point during the abduction — that he was going to march the mayor around the state. Navajo college students who are politically active tend to talk more than other young demonstrators do about shame and dignity and ridicule. In planning the protest march at the 1971 Gallup Ceremonial, they decided to have two demonstrators ride on horseback partly on the theory that men riding above the crowd on horses were more difficult to ridicule. When they talk about having Gallup on the run, they sometimes say that Indians are now "snickering at Gallup." "Larry wanted to show the people that the mayor deserved no respect," a Navajo girl at the Kiva Club said later. "Larry wanted to humiliate him, to bring him down to the people's level. For a long time, the Indian people have believed that white men are better than they are. The mayor was an authority figure. I think Larry would have taken him out and walked him through the streets of Gallup — to show it was just a man, to show that the Indian people should be treated with respect."

REPORTER: *Did they indicate what their grief was with the mayor?*
DERIZOTIS: *No, sir, not at all.*

A lot of Gallup residents thought of the mayor, Emmet (Frankie) Garcia, as what used to be called a real go-getter — an energetic, ambitious, pragmatic young man who was the first person to treat the mayor's office as a full-time job. He had hired some people from outside Gallup and had tried to take advantage of any federal money that was available. He had helped organize an alcoholism project — working against the inclination of Gallup citizens to believe that Indian alcoholism is an Indian problem, even if the alcohol is provided in Gallup — and had rounded up financial support from the city and the county and the state in anticipation of a large federal grant for a rehabilitation center. He had served all but a few weeks of his first two-year term, and his reëlection seemed almost certain.

To Larry Casuse, Frankie Garcia was the man who presided over a town that enriched itself on Indians — on their trade, on their artistic talents, on their ceremonies, on their drinking. Even worse, he was a part owner of the Navajo Inn, a package liquor store a few hundred feet from the Navajo reservation. The Navajo Inn is a small cinder-block building surrounded by open space and on some paydays by so many passed-out Navajos that it takes on the appearance of a bunker in a recently contested battlefield. Frankie Garcia had said that, as one-third owner, he had no control over the way the Navajo Inn was run. He had also argued at times that a liquor store next to the reservation was less dangerous than one in Gallup, twenty-five miles away — the difference being how many miles a Navajo had to drive drunk to get home. It is possible to argue, of course, that the Navajo Inn, however grotesque and callous and ugly it might be, is not the real headquarters of the enemy, any more than a Jewish pawn-broker on 125th Street is the real agent of the miseries afflicting black people in Harlem — that blaming the Navajo Inn for the alcoholism problem is no more accurate than blaming tribal prohibition or the Navajo bootleggers who support it. But if the Navajo Inn is only a symptom of the condition the Navajos find themselves in, it is a particularly visible and profitable symptom, and the one most despised among Navajos, who have seen many of their people destroy themselves with alcohol. According to Frankie Garcia, the Navajo Inn, a cinder-block hut miles from the nearest large town, has steadily been the single most profitable liquor store in the state of New Mexico.

Larry Casuse and his friends had become increasingly interested in the traditional Navajo way of thought — a way of life based on man's living in harmony with all that surrounds him. Casuse had written poems and fables about the harm brought by change. He had spent some time talking to Navajo medicine men, and had spoken to his mother about wanting to go back to the reservation to live simply in the traditional Navajo way. He and his friends seemed particularly taken with a concept of "false people" — people who pretend to understand but actually are so lacking in the compassion and sensitivity inherent in the Navajo way that they have a questionable claim on being human beings. Frankie Garcia, who was chairman of an alcoholism project while profiteering from Indian drinking, was their prime example of a false person. Despite that, the governor of New Mexico had, in January, appointed Frankie Garcia to the University of New Mexico Board of Regents.

REPORTER: *A man has apparently just been shot and thrown out the window. We can't tell at this time if it is the mayor. . . . Another shot has been fired . . . and another shot. . . . Chief Gonzales has a rifle.*

The University of New Mexico student newspaper printed some editorials critical of Garcia's appointment. The student senate, after hearing a speech about the appointment's being a political payoff and watching while a doll representing Garcia was burned, passed a resolution calling for "a more qualified and suitable candidate." But the strongest opposition was from the Kiva Club, and particularly from its president, Larry Casuse. When Garcia's nomination came before the Rules Committee of the New Mexico Senate, Casuse and some other students went to Santa Fe to testify against it. Casuse had gathered documents and photographs and had circulated a petition. "The man is an owner of the Navajo Inn, where numerous alcoholics are born, yet he ironically is chairman of the alcohol-abuse rehabilitation committee," Casuse told the senators. "Does he not abuse alcohol? Does he not abuse it by selling it to intoxicated persons who often end up in jail or in a morgue from overexposure?" The nomination was approved by the committee — "They were just like stone-faced men," one of the students said — and then by the Senate.

When Garcia was about to be sworn in, at a regents' meeting held on the U.N.M. campus in Albuquerque, Casuse stood to ask permission to make a statement, and the permission was politely granted. Casuse spoke of the charges he had made against Garcia and of the lack of interest exhibited by the senators. "These are the type of people who run our government, and these aren't The People — these are the false people," he said. "There's no reason for me to scream or shout. There's no reason for me to bring documents. There's no reason, because you people will just turn your head, like you always turn your head. There's no reason for that. So what we're going to do is, we're going to find all the human beings in this country, in this state, and we're going to get the human beings together and we're going to put an end to people like Emmet Garcia, and we're going to start with Emmet Garcia. We don't really care what you people do. Because you people aren't human beings."

Casuse sat down, and there was scattered applause from his supporters, and the chairman said, "The second item on the agenda is the swearing in."

REPORTER: *City Manager Paul McCollum, can you give us a report on the mayor's condition?*

McCOLLUM: *He is all right. . . . He came out through the window. . . .*

REPORTER: *Do you know at this time what the grievance is?*

McCOLLUM: *I have no idea at this point of time what the grievance might be.*

REPORTER: *Do you know why they released him?*

McCOLLUM: *I think that he must have escaped himself. . . .*

REPORTER: *Shots are continuing to be fired from out of Stearn's Sporting Goods. . . . What appears to be a tear-gas bomb has just been shot into Stearn's Sporting Goods. . . .*

VOICE: *They're going to come out shooting.*

REPORTER: *They're coming out with their hands on their head. One of them thus far has come out. . . . He has been directed by the officers to lie flat. . . . His partner in hav-*

ing taken the mayor hostage remains in Stearn's Sporting Goods store. . . . Police are now pouring into the Stearn's Sporting Goods store. . . . They have now dragged out what appears to be Larry Wayne Casuse. He is covered with blood. . . . I am approaching the body. . . . From a distance of about thirty feet, Larry Wayne Casuse appears to be dead.

VOICE: *Get a blanket.*

Eventually, someone did get a blanket. But Larry Casuse's body lay uncovered on the sidewalk in front of Stearn's Sporting Goods store for a while — long enough for the local paper to take a picture of it with three police standing over it like hunters who had just bagged their seasonal deer. It is now speculated that the appearance of the picture on the front page of the *Gallup Independent* may have had a lot to do with the outrage expressed even by Navajos who ordinarily have no interest in politics and no sympathy for the activist students of Indians Against Exploitation. For whatever reason, it soon became apparent that the incident had made an extraordinary impact on all sorts of Navajos. A white with wide contacts on the reservation said later, "People I had expected to say 'Well, he asked for it' said the only thing they couldn't understand is why he didn't kill the mayor when he had a chance." The elected chairman of the Navajo Tribal Council, Peter McDonald, a Nixon Republican who had never been a supporter of the militant young people, at first responded to the incident by expressing his shock and sending his sympathies to Garcia, but by the time Larry Casuse's funeral was held, McDonald had decided to be among the mourners. When the *Albuquerque Journal* did a long piece on the aftermath of Casuse's death, some of the harshest statements about the city of Gallup gathered by its reporter, Scott Beaven, were from the kind of Indians most despised by the young activists — middle-aged Indians who work for the local government or the Bureau of Indian Affairs. A Gallup protest march Casuse had helped organize on Thanksgiving Day had drawn a hundred and twenty-five young people; a march four weeks after his death attracted a couple of thousand Indians of all ages.

Gallup officials said Larry Casuse had shot himself, although they also said that a bullet wound inflicted by the police would have killed him anyway. Some white sympathizers thought suicide was a possibility — "After all, the whole thing was suicidal," one of them said — but Casuse's Navajo friends said suicide was out of the question, since it was contrary to the Navajo beliefs he had come to hold important. A flyer announcing a march just after his death was headed "Was Larry Casuse Murdered?," and some Indian groups demanded an investigation. But a statement from the Kiva Club — addressed to "All Human Beings" — said, "The real issue is not who-shot-whom, as the national media seem to imply, but rather why Larry Casuse so willingly sacrificed his life in order to communicate with the world his dream of unifying human beings with Mother Earth, the Universe, and Humanity."

You Always Turn Your Head

REPORTER: *There is speculation that the mayor has been wounded, but he has been taken to his family and is apparently all right.*

The mayor's injuries — a shotgun wound and some cuts incurred when he leaped out of the window — were minor, and it appeared that the incident could only enhance his political career, there being no significant Navajo vote in Gallup. Some citizens were concerned that the shooting might shift the attention of the American Indian Movement from Wounded Knee to Gallup, but Garcia removed the most obvious focus for a demonstration by buying controlling interest in the Navajo Inn and announcing, after a meeting with local Indian groups, that he would close it for thirty days. He made it clear that during the closing he would either sell the store to the tribe at a reasonable price so that it could be closed permanently or move the license into Gallup.

To the surprise of just about everyone, Frankie Garcia lost the election. The defeat is now usually explained as having been caused by Garcia's apparent reluctance to campaign and by the possibility that Gallup voters had begun to associate Garcia with Indian trouble and figured the trouble might stop if he was no longer there to provoke it. Garcia himself singles out the huge Indian march on the Saturday before the election as the most damaging factor in the campaign. The people in Gallup who were working for an alcoholism-rehabilitation center tend to believe that there is less chance of having one with Garcia no longer present to push the project, although the general cutback in federal funds for such programs made the prospect of an elaborate center highly unlikely anyway. The tribe could still buy the Navajo Inn, but Garcia now sees no reason to accept anything but a good price for it. If a profitable arrangement cannot be made with the tribe, Garcia told a visitor recently, he plans to leave the Navajo Inn right where it is and make as much money as possible from it. "I've gone strictly business now," he said. In that spirit, he has decided to resign from the University of New Mexico Board of Regents.

Harvey St. Jean
Had It Made

Miami Beach, Florida
March 1975

CRIMINAL LAWYERS are not the kind of lawyers who claim to be just as happy if their names never appear in a newspaper. One guide to how well a criminal lawyer is doing, in fact, may be how many times he is mentioned in the newspapers and in what size type — the criminal case that attracts the attention of the press often being one in which the defendant is important enough to be able to pay his attorney. A top criminal lawyer has his biography written serially in the tabloids. In the private office of Harvey St. Jean, by all accounts the top criminal lawyer in Miami Beach, the wall decorations were not just framed diplomas but framed newspaper clippings. His outer office had the Spy caricatures of English judges that most American lawyers must receive from their wives most Christmases, but it also had a series of originals by a local newspaper artist who had drawn the lawyer in the courtroom scenes as a tall, imposing man with gray hair and heavy black eyebrows — Harvey St. Jean. St. Jean had plenty of clients who made the front page of the Miami papers. ("'I'm so happy,' cries Mrs. Shirley Mae Lewis Tuesday after a circuit-court jury acquitted her in the murder of a Miami Beach widow. Donald C. Bliss pleaded guilty Monday to the stabbing of Mrs. Ruth Berkman and accused Mrs. Lewis of handing him the knife.") He also had clients whose fate was of importance to newspapers in Philadelphia and New York. For years, St. Jean was in the papers as the attorney for people who had become familiar enough to be given nicknames, the way halfbacks and middleweights are given nicknames. The Crying Adjmis, for instance, a family of bric-a-brac hustlers accused (and acquitted) of bilking a rich widow out of half a million dollars with the help of a phony French priest who said that only the widow's money could save his orphanage and village from a greedy German named Finklestein. ("I was a softie," the victim acknowledged.) Jack (Murph the Surf) Murphy, who, with a couple of other Miami beachboys, managed to steal the Star of India sapphire and the deLong Star Ruby from the American Museum of Natural History and pass the ruby along — or so the government alleged — to Richard Duncan Pearson, another client of Harvey St. Jean. The widow of Arthur (Fat Man) Blatt, who became a widow by putting five bullets into the Fat Man, a jeweller by trade and someone suspected by the police for a while of having the deLong

Ruby in his inventory. And Candy — Candace Mossler, who was accused of having arranged with her nephew Melvin Powers to beat her millionaire husband to death with a large Coke bottle. Candy hired both Percy Foreman and Harvey St. Jean to argue her innocence. The fruits of their triumph included a wire-service picture of Candy kissing St. Jean in appreciation and a huge acquittal headline on the front page of that final law journal for big-time criminal attorneys — the *New York Daily News.*

"Harvey St. Jean had it made," Edna Buchanan and Gene Miller began their front-page story in the *Miami Herald* December 12th. "He had money, a reputation as a crack criminal lawyer, and time to tee off for 18 holes at La Gorce Country Club any afternoon he wanted. Most afternoons he did.

"When he left his apartment at the Jockey Club Wednesday morning . . . he had his golf clubs in the trunk of his Cadillac. Wednesday looked like an easy day. He figured he might pick up a game later with Eddie Arcaro, the jockey. He didn't.

"In the crisp bright light of Miami Beach, someone murdered him. He was found shot to death in his car."

Harvey St. Jean started his Miami Beach career digging ditches for the city — a poor boy from Holyoke, Massachusetts, whose résumé could not have gone much beyond some clippings of high-school athletic triumphs. It was 1939, with the Depression still on in most of the country. "People came here because things weren't right where they came from," Bernard Wieder, a Miami Beach lawyer who had been St. Jean's friend and fellow-ditchdigger in those days, said recently. "This was pioneer country." Some of the pioneers were just drifters; some were ambitious. One of the people who dug ditches with St. Jean and Wieder became president of the bank in whose aqua high rise, on the Lincoln Road Mall, both of them eventually practiced law. Another was elected mayor of Miami Beach. St. Jean and Wieder both took the examinations to become policemen — a seasonal occupation then — and firemen. Wieder still has an early picture of them as policemen at the Miami Beach version of a community event — a wedding of Bernarr Macfadden, the health faddist. St. Jean saved a picture of himself in police uniform standing behind a posed meeting of Jake LaMotta, Rocky Graziano, and Walter Winchell.

In 1951 — when, after years of holding down a regular police job and attending law school at the same time, St. Jean was admitted to the bar — a lot of people considered the practice of criminal law to be a step down from practically anything. The leading criminal lawyer in Miami Beach owed his preëminence to being the favored attorney for members of the S. & G. Syndicate, which used to control the gambling in south Florida. Many of his colleagues at the criminal bar were considered hacks or shysters. There are now criminal lawyers who spend a lot of their time defending sophisticated businessmen charged with tax evasion, but criminal lawyers are still not quite respectable in the sense that, say, specialists in trusts or corporate mergers are respectable. Their clients are usually not the kind of people with whom it would be appropriate to discuss the case over luncheon at a decent club. There is often talk of fees paid in stolen goods or of chumminess with mobsters. "To a professional detective, any criminal attorney has to be a certain part fixer," a professional detective with the Miami Beach force said recently. When Harvey St. Jean was already the leading criminal attorney in Miami and was expanding into some business ventures, those city councilmen who argued, unsuccessfully, against awarding him the contract to run the concessions at the city golf course based their argument on the kind of undesirables he defended and might associate with in business. Like any two groups of people thrown together, criminal lawyers and their clientele sometimes develop complicated links of style, or even of family. One of St. Jean's associates was once married to a woman who had previously been married to one of St. Jean's clients. One of St. Jean's own wives — he had a number of them — was once married to a man identified as a close associate of Frank Costello. She almost became some criminal lawyer's client herself — so St. Jean said during the divorce case — by pointing a gun at him and pulling the trigger twice on what happened to be empty chambers.

Even people who assume all criminal lawyers to be part fixer refer to Harvey St. Jean as a gentleman. He was a soft-spoken man, closemouthed about important matters but affable about routine ones. People who had known him for years could not recall ever hearing him raise his voice. The judges liked him, and so did the police. As someone who had been a policeman for years himself, he had friends on the force who could steer clients in his direction, and he could translate the stilted jargon of police reports into some vision of what must have really happened. He steadily worked his way up from pickpockets to jewel thieves. St. Jean was never an eloquent or flamboyant man — tables went unpounded and tears went unshed during his summations — but he was shrewd about picking juries and thorough about rules of evidence that often made it possible to exclude from consideration the statement or the jewelry necessary for a prosecution. As the Warren Court decisions increasingly emphasized the rights of the individual, criminal law was increasingly practiced not with eloquent summations but with detailed challenges to the affidavit that led to a search warrant or with hard questions about how the defendant was treated at the station house. Harvey St. Jean became what his partner, Lawrence Hoffman, believes was the finest search-and-seizure lawyer in the country.

As his practice grew and some real-estate investments began to pay off, St. Jean began to lead the south-Florida version of life at the top. There may be cities in which the respectability of a self-made criminal lawyer will always have its limits, but in Miami just about everyone seems to have a tenuous hold on respectability anyway. The historic attraction of the

area for promoters and grifters and profligates being
what it is, Miami remains a hard place to cash a check.
The difference between an established family and a
new family sometimes seems to be that the established
family pulled off some successful land-flipping in the
thirties instead of the fifties. The dominant standard
of a club like the Jockey Club — often described
around town as "the 'in' place" or "a swinging joint"
or "the place to be" — is ready money, and motivation
by money is assumed. (Some pieces of African sculp-
ture for sale in a showcase are identified as "Rare Col-
lector's Items for Investors in African Art.") The golf
club that elected Harvey St. Jean to its board of governors — La Gorce Country Club, in Miami Beach —
had, according to an estimate in the *Miami Herald* a
few years ago, five hundred millionaires among eleven
hundred members, including a Firestone and a du Pont.
It had the final badge of exclusivity in Miami Beach:
it excluded Jews, like the one British planters' club in
a newly independent African country that can't bring
itself to alter its membership rules enough to allow in
the new president. But La Gorce was not founded until
after the Second World War. And one of its members
was accused by the Internal Revenue Service a few
years ago of having used it as a base for hustling some
five hundred thousand unreported dollars from golf
or poker patsies, and a *Herald* story about changes in
its board of governors a couple of years ago described
one of them as "auto dealer, former state senator, and
sometime associate of bookmakers."

In the past several years, anyone looking for Harvey St. Jean was likely to find him at La Gorce or the Jockey Club or in his office — and his office became, increasingly, the least likely of the three. In 1970, St. Jean had an operation for some old knee injuries — the Miami Dolphins team surgeon was his doctor — and, still in his fifties, he began to tell people he was semi-retired. He spent a lot of time on the golf course and on various business ventures. A couple of times a year, he went to the Golden Door spa in California. "He just said he was semi-retired as a way to avoid the wise guys who wanted him to do small cases for nothing," Jack Nageley, a Miami Beach criminal lawyer who once worked for St. Jean, has said. "If there was enough money involved, Harvey was there." The money was in the occasional big criminal trial and, more and more, in the divorce work brought in by his fame or by his contacts with rich and important people.

A divorce lawyer who lived at the Jockey Club could feel as secure about his future as a dentist who lived in Hershey, Pennsylvania. The standing joke at the Jockey Club is that the average age of the residents is forty — "that's a sixty-year-old guy and a twenty-year-old broad." The club consists of a couple of high rises full of condominiums for the live-in members, some tennis courts, a marina in which some of the boats seem large enough to serve as destroyer escorts, a restaurant, and a bar whose patrons are so uniformly the type of people who order drinks by brand ("J & B and a twist, Joe, and an extra-dry Tanqueray Martini") that the bartender's reaction to being asked for a Scotch-and-soda is likely to be a moment of puzzlement, as if he had just been asked for a jug of homemade busthead. The Jockey Club is a place in which the names dropped at the bar are vaguely familiar — familiar because the people were once in films or because their families have even more money than they can spend on boats and alimony payments — and the names displayed on the membership invitations seem designed to trigger the same kind of brand identification as modish brands of gin. Twenty-five years after he stood anonymously behind Walter Winchell, Harvey St. Jean lived, with his wife, in a condominium at a club whose board of governors includes Perry Como and Pierre du Pont and Fess Parker. He owned two condominiums at the Jockey Club, in fact, having moved into a larger one after his marriage and held on to his bachelor apartment. He had been talking about trying to consolidate their mortgages. He apparently had a cash-flow problem. But he had sent a check to the condominium sales office at the Cricket Club, which is being built just north of the Jockey Club. The Cricket Club will have a full spa, and many people believe that it will be the new place to live.

Walter Philbin looks and talks enough like a detective to play one in the movies — and has played one, several times. In "Lenny," the New York detective sergeant who arrested Bruce at a night club and then testified, with some embarrassment, in court as to his language and gestures was played by Walter Philbin. In real life, he is a major, the chief of detectives of the Miami Beach Police Department, and in real life he had some dealings with Lenny Bruce. ("I harassed him pretty good.") Philbin joined the Miami Beach force the year after Harvey St. Jean left — another poor boy from Massachusetts. "We more or less grew up together — me on the force, him in the practice of law," Philbin said recently. "I beat him on ten or eleven first-degree-murder cases. I was his nemesis." St. Jean won some, too. "I once collared a guy on a stakeout with two hundred thousand dollars in stolen jewels — *and a gun*," Philbin says. "Harvey got him off on search-and-seizure." Philbin believes that he and Harvey St. Jean exchanged the respect of competent adversaries, and he recalls thinking about that when he arrived at a public parking lot between the Lincoln Road Mall and the Convention Center late on a Wednesday morning last December and found St. Jean shot to death inside his Cadillac. "When we were taking him out of the car, it was a funny thing to think about, but I thought Harvey would be glad that if anyone had to investigate his murder it would be me — because I think he had respect for me as a homicide investigator," Philbin said. "It was an almost communicative feeling: 'Don't worry about it, Harvey.' And him saying, 'Well, I'm glad you're here, because if anybody can get the son of a bitch, you can.' "

There may be detectives who would regard that as the recollection of a member of the Screen Actors Guild, but any homicide investigator would sympathize with the next thought Philbin recalls having: "Jesus, God! He's got a hundred guys capable of killing him." A disgruntled client? An ex-wife? One of the undesirables that people said St. Jean had as associates in his business ventures? A hit man from the mob? Just a thief who heard that St. Jean often carried a lot of cash with him? Philbin's detectives fairly quickly eliminated the possibility of random robbery, and turned up only one undesirable and no strong suspects among St. Jean's business associates. ("I almost wish I could talk to Harvey: 'How could you get involved with this creep?'") The street talk and the prison grapevine produced a theory about St. Jean's murder almost immediately: that he had been killed on the orders of a Cuban cocaine dealer, a former client, who believed St. Jean had a lot of his money and was refusing to return it. The theory was consistent with some of the physical evidence, Philbin thought, such as the fact that St. Jean had been robbed. ("It's a matter of honor with an Italian hit man not to touch anything; Cubans rob the guy as part of the deal — the price plus what he's carrying.") It was the theory in newspaper headlines within a day or two of the shooting, and it remains the dominant theory in the Police Department today, even though Walter Philbin, for one, is not optimistic about ever finding enough evidence to indict whoever it was who actually pulled the trigger.

Since the St. Jean killing, Philbin has arrived at some strong views on the version of organized crime that has developed among post-Castro Cuban immigrants. He believes that Cuban gangsters often behave the way Italian gangsters did in the twenties, when they had been in the country only fifteen or twenty years themselves — extorting money from their own community's businessmen, for instance, and shooting at each other a lot in arguments over power. The Cubans differ, he believes, in concentrating on a type of business that some of the old-style immigrant gangsters avoided — drugs. The people in charge of Cuban organized crime learned organization from the American gangsters who were in Cuba at the end of the Batista regime, Philbin thinks, and the eighteen- and twenty-year-olds now used as runners and enforcers learned how to be hoods right in the United States of America. "When the Cubans first came here, we'd always say they were no trouble," Philbin said recently. "Strong family ties. Strong culture. Now, eighteen, nineteen years later, we got nothing but trouble. They've lost their strong family ties, they've lost their strong culture. And the sad thing is that *we've* done it. We've Americanized them. They learned everything on our streets." The organized Cuban operation that uses the street toughs, Philbin thinks, is much more powerful than has been believed. Among the people who may have underestimated the Cubans was Harvey St. Jean.

Why the client in question believed that St. Jean owed him money remains a matter of conjecture, of course. There is a theory, expressed in the newspapers by Dade County State Attorney Richard Gerstein, that "some of those people just assume that if they pay large fees they are buying a dismissal or acquittal." There is a theory that St. Jean, a controlled and unemotional man in the courtroom, might have exacerbated such a misunderstanding by carrying on a defense that could have seemed unenergetic to a Latin. It is possible, of course, that the money that changed hands really was for services other than the defense of one case. It is even possible that Harvey St. Jean, a secretive man with a cash-flow problem, really did keep some money he should have returned. "Harvey had almost scrupulously avoided drug cases," Philbin says. "He was doing pretty well without them. But this was so much money he couldn't turn it down." The amount usually mentioned is something over a hundred thousand dollars. "Harvey knew all the angles," Jack Nageley said not long ago. "But his love of money did him in."

Harvey St. Jean made banner headlines with his funeral. "The friends of Harvey St. Jean, the honest ones, assembled before an open casket Saturday for piped organ music — and the prayers of a priest who never met him," Gene Miller wrote in the *Herald*. "It was simple and quick. Only the last of his seven wives attended. Detectives saw none of his notorious clients. Harvey J. St. Jean, criminal lawyer, is now case number 385393." In a short eulogy, a friend called St. Jean "a sportsman and a sport." His widow, Dorothy St. Jean, got a lot of sympathy letters from important people and ordinary people, and even some people who wrote from prison — the type of client she could remember her husband's considering "a thief, but a nice thief." She also got the cash-flow problem. She is a bright, red-haired woman who, like her husband, came to Miami Beach poor, twenty years ago — a secretary from New Jersey. She worked her way up from a cocktail-waitress job to a job at one of the big hotels organizing conventions and Super Bowl charters. Last fall, she had quit her job and devoted her organizing energies to charity work. She was having lunch at La Gorce when she heard of her husband's death. One of the ironies she mentions when she talks about the murder is that she and Harvey St. Jean, two people who had worked their way up, finally had it made. "People came up afterward and said, 'At least, his problems are over now,'" she said recently. "Listen. He didn't have any problems."

Partners

New England
October 1975

SEABROOK, NEW HAMPSHIRE, has the look of those towns that have grown up over the years along Route 1 the way algae sometimes grow along a ship's line that has been left underwater too long. It is just across the state line from Massachusetts, near New Hampshire's short stretch of Atlantic shore, and Bostonians of a certain age tend to associate it with quickie-marriage factories — an industrial base that has long since been supplanted by a dog track. In Seabrook, Route 1 is dominated by the type of sign that seems to have been created by mounting the side of an old-fashioned theatre marquee on a portable iron frame that can be wheeled to the roadside to attract the attention of a highway driver whose eye may not have wandered far enough to be caught by the signs on the gift shops and farm stands and factory outlets that lie just beyond the blacktop parking lots on either side of the road. All of the iron frames are painted yellow, and a lot of them include a huge yellow arrow curving back to point across the parking lot, and some of the arrows are outlined in multicolored blinking light bulbs. The Hawaiian Garden restaurant and lounge, which specializes in "Cantonese-Polynesian Food & Drinks," is right on Route 1, with a parking lot on the side and some motel rooms in a connecting building along the back. Its restaurant serves the sort of Polynesian food that would be familiar to any Samoan or Fijian who happened to have eaten at a Trader Vic's outlet, as well as fourteen varieties of chow mein. Its lounge — a more ambitiously decorated room than the restaurant, with a large bandstand and ersatz tikis and a straw-mat ceiling over the bar — has a repertoire of drinks that makes it the only place on that stretch of Route 1 for someone who feels the need of a pick-me-up that comes in a ceramic coconut and is decorated with a tiny paper umbrella. The co-proprietor of the Hawaiian Garden — the man out in front, not the one in the kitchen — is a Cantonese immigrant named Wing Chin, who came with his family to Providence as a teenager in the fifties and, in the tradition of Chinese-American entrepreneurship, spent some time working as a waiter in other people's restaurants before opening his own. Last year, after operating the Hawaiian Garden for seven or eight years, Wing Chin became one of four partners in a corporation formed to establish another Cantonese-Polynesian restaurant, just outside Atlanta, Georgia, in a town called Marietta — a town that does not have a dog track but does have a large aircraft factory. Each of the four partners agreed to put up twenty thousand dollars, the First National Bank of Boston agreed to lend the new corporation one hundred and sixty-six thousand dollars, the Small Business Administration committed itself to guaranteeing the loan, and a contract was signed for a building in Marietta. Wing Chin remembers saying to his partners, "I don't think we can miss."

The one silent partner in Chin Enterprises, Incorporated, was the type of investor often found in such ventures, a relative of Wing Chin's who was always referred to by the active partners as Uncle Harry. The president of the new corporation was Wing Chin, the only partner who had extensive experience in the restaurant business. The vice-president, a boyhood friend of Chin's named John Oi, had been a busboy in a Chinese restaurant as a teenager — it was there that he met Chin, who was working as a waiter — but otherwise his restaurant background was one generation removed. His father, Henry Oi, was a restaurant proprietor who was also a prominent member of the Boston Chinatown business community — a man who, starting as an impoverished immigrant from Canton, had become proprietor first of a Cantonese-Polynesian restaurant in Boston and then of two more in Connecticut. John Oi, though, was not a restaurant proprietor but a professional soldier — a Regular Army captain who had graduated from West Point and happened to be back in the Boston area during the formation of Chin Enterprises, Incorporated, only because the Army had sent him to Northeastern University to complete a master's degree in electrical engineering. His wife, Cheryl, who came from a Chinese family in Hawaii, had a doctorate in ethnomusicology and ran an Asian program for one of the Boston television stations. Together, living in an apartment complex in the southwest suburbs, they seemed a long way from the Chinese immigrants working in the steamy kitchens of Chinatown. When a local reporter asked their neighbors for a description of John and Cheryl Oi some time later, what he wrote down was "Very friendly, always seemed busy, highly educated, classy." They apparently looked on the Marietta restaurant as an investment that might eventually turn into a vocation — a place they might go to someday if John decided to leave the service after putting in twenty years. John Oi said nothing about the investment to his father. In a way, John had fulfilled the traditional role of the son of an ambitious immigrant in America. Henry Oi — who, despite imperfect English and no American education, had managed to get into flight school and become an officer in the Second World War — had been given the opportunity to swear in his son as a second lieutenant at a West Point commencement. But, according to Cheryl Oi, the Marietta restaurant was partly a way for her husband to prove himself to his father as a businessman as well as a soldier — as a successful partner in precisely the same kind of restaurant that Henry Oi operated. "I knew nothing about it," Henry Oi said recently. "If I had, I would have knocked holes in it."

Henry Oi, who had slept on the office floor rather than leave his West Hartford restaurant during its first weeks of operation, might have questioned the wisdom of opening a restaurant so far away. Restaurants may be even more in need of constant supervision than other retail cash businesses, and restaurant proprietors, like commanders of armies in the field, are ordinarily cautious about straying too far from their support operations. As a veteran of the tightly knit ventures of Boston's Chinatown, Henry Oi would also have presumably been put off by the fact that the fourth partner in Chin Enterprises, Incorporated, was an Occidental — a former New Hampshire state policeman named Armand R. Therrien. A contemporary of Wing Chin and John Oi, Therrien was the son of a lumberjack from the center of New Hampshire — a descendant of the poor French Canadians who had come to New England from rural Quebec to work in the forests and the mills, and, for the most part, had remained poor. After a few years in the Air Force, Armand Therrien had worked as a Northeast Airlines ticket agent for five years and then joined the state police, where he showed an aptitude for investigating crimes like embezzlement. He was eventually made a detective corporal and assigned to an office near Seabrook, a hundred miles from his home. In 1973, he resigned from the state police, moved permanently to Seabrook, and began trying to make a living as an insurance agent. "I wanted to better myself," he said later. He had been divorced the previous year, and he had two households to support. Selling insurance did not turn out to be the route to quick riches, nor did selling real estate. In the synopsis of a résumé Therrien composed at the time, he wrote, "Schooling limited. Capabilities unlimited. Ambition strong. Training varied and diversified. I have enjoyed and done well at all my occupations but to date have not found one that would consume my entire efforts." Therrien had known Wing Chin since the late sixties, when, as a state trooper, he was in the habit of dropping by the Hawaiian Garden — or "the Gardens," as he came to call it. During 1973, he began to work for Chin — first part-time as a sort of security man for the lounge, and then full-time as just about everything except chef and bartender. Therrien lived at the Gardens; his girl friend was one of the waitresses. He made some junkets to Las Vegas. But he was regular about his checks to his family and regular about Sunday visits to his children. Therrien was not only the secretary-treasurer of Chin Enterprises, Incorporated, but the only partner who planned to work as a salaried employee at the Marietta restaurant — as the manager. John Oi and Wing Chin apparently saw Therrien in the role of a sort of white front man in Georgia. The three partners spent a lot of time together in the summer of 1974 — planning the Marietta restaurant, hunting, target shooting in a quarry near the Gardens. In January of this year, John and Cheryl Oi took Therrien and his girl friend to an Italian restaurant in Boston for a farewell dinner before Therrien left to supervise renovation of the building in Georgia. As Cheryl Oi remembers that evening, the only business conversation was some jovial talk about who would buy the first Rolls-Royce after Chin Enterprises, Incorporated, hit the jackpot.

On February 11th, in Westwood, a Boston suburb a few miles from where John and Cheryl Oi lived, Patrolmen William Sheehan and Robert P. O'Donnell were partners for the four-to-midnight shift, riding in Police Cruiser 92. Bill Sheehan, the senior member of the Westwood Police Department, was known as an amiable and conscientious man who had personally broken in many of the officers on the force. A widower, he often worked nights, and occasionally picked up some extra money doing lawn care during the day. Sheehan's father had been a caretaker on an estate; one of his brothers was a fireman. His daughter was a graduate of Boston College, and his son was a senior at Dartmouth. Sheehan was working that evening — a bitterly cold and occasionally snowy evening — with the most junior member of the force, O'Donnell having been appointed only a month before. A clean-cut, rather laconic man in his late twenties, O'Donnell, like his father before him, had been an ironworker — putting together the girders of Boston high rises for ten years before turning to an occupation he expected to be both more satisfying and more secure than work in the steadily narrowing construction field. As O'Donnell remembers the events of February 11th, he and Bill Sheehan turned onto Canton Street, a wooded but heavily travelled road that feeds onto Route 128, at about seven-thirty and saw a Pontiac Grand Prix parked a few feet from the curb, with its emergency lights flashing. The driver, as seen in silhouette through the fogged window, seemed slumped in his seat. Parking the cruiser and walking back toward the Grand Prix, Sheehan and O'Donnell were met by a man dressed in fatigues, who had come out of the passenger side to say that his friend was ill but no help was needed. The two policemen, suspecting a drunk driver, continued to the Grand Prix and looked in. "Hey, what's all the blood?" O'Donnell said. Someone said "Hey," there was a blinding flash as O'Donnell turned, and he felt himself falling. There were more shots, and then O'Donnell, feeling a foot next to him, grabbed at it and began struggling with the man in fatigues, only to have him break loose and run. O'Donnell drew his own gun and fired, bringing the man down in the middle of Canton Street. As it turned out, O'Donnell had two minor wounds and serious powder burns of the face. Bill Sheehan lay dying on the street, a bullet from a snub-nosed .38 in his head. The man slumped in the driver's seat had a similar .38 slug in the head, and died not long after reaching the hospital. He was identified as Captain John Oi. The man in fatigues was Armand Therrien. His wounds were not critical, and the following morning, in Massachusetts General Hospital, a Westwood police officer was able to inform him that he was being charged with the murder of John Oi. "He was my business partner," Therrien said to the police officer.

*

"The word 'probably' is not enough," Therrien's defense attorney, a well-known criminal lawyer from
Boston named Gerald Alch, said as he explained the
concept of "reasonable doubt" during Therrien's trial
for the murders of John Oi and William Sheehan. No
one had actually seen Oi and Sheehan shot, but the
circumstantial evidence seemed overwhelming. The
bullets that killed both victims had been fired by the
.38 Therrien was carrying. A box of shells and two
pairs of handcuffs had been found in Therrien's pocket.
A room key, also found in his pocket, had led to the
discovery that he had checked into a nearby motel that
afternoon under an assumed name, after a virtually
non-stop drive from Georgia. The telephone in his
apartment in Marietta had been left off the hook, and
when he telephoned his girl friend in New Hampshire
during the drive north he had given her the impression
that he was still in Georgia, with no plans to leave.
The police reasoned that Therrien, having parked his
own car in a restaurant lot near John Oi's apartment,
was forcing Oi to drive him toward a deserted spot
when Oi, perhaps with thoughts of escape, suddenly
stopped the car on Canton Street — only to be shot in
the back of the head. But why? In the day or two after
Oi's death, the police received a couple of anonymous
tips that the crime had to do with gambling and the
mob; the district attorney was quoted in the local press
as saying that the investigation was partly concerned
with the possibility that Therrien was connected with
"the Chinese Mafia." Then police discovered that Chin

Enterprises, Incorporated, had, as a requirement of its loan, taken out a two-hundred-thousand-dollar life-insurance policy on each of its officers — policies that were to be assigned to the bank as soon as the final loan papers were signed. Oi's death at a time when the policies were payable directly to Chin Enterprises, Incorporated, meant that the restaurant would be capitalized with an additional two hundred thousand dollars. The corporation would have no need to take a bank loan and operate under its restrictions — which included a limit of fifteen thousand dollars a year on salaries that could be drawn by corporate officers. Neither Oi nor Chin was concerned with salary because Chin had the Hawaiian Garden and Oi had the Army, the prosecutor, an assistant district attorney named John P. Connor, Jr., told the jury. "But Therrien cared. Because Therrien wanted to better himself."

Therrien's trial was in the courthouse at Dedham, the seat of Norfolk County. Bill Sheehan's son and daughter were there, and so was Henry Oi. Cheryl Oi and Wing Chin were among those called to testify by the prosecution. Armand Therrien's sisters and his girl friend and his former wife were all among the spectators — all loyal, all willing to demonstrate by their presence that those closest to Therrien believed he could never have committed the crimes he was charged with. Except for one moment, when he broke into tears while reading a letter he had sent Henry Oi from jail, Therrien was calm and self-assured on the stand — still enough of a policeman to refer to O'Donnell as "the subject." He offered four or five legitimate reasons to explain his sudden trip north. He said that his girl friend had been allowed to believe he was still in Georgia because he wanted to surprise her. The gun was with him because he was returning it to its owner in New Hampshire, and the handcuffs and shells happened to be in the pocket of his heavy coat because he had been cleaning out his desk at the Gardens the last time he was in a cold enough place to wear it. He had registered under an assumed name at the motel because he happened to have a female hitchhiker with him at the time. Therrien said he couldn't remember everything that had happened on Canton Street that night because Oi had hit him during an argument that began with Oi's insisting that Wing Chin was heavily in debt from gambling and was planning to cheat his partners in Chin Enterprises, Incorporated. As Therrien told it, Oi had apparently been shot accidentally during an argument with O'Donnell, who then turned on Sheehan. It was a story that offered some explanation for every piece of incriminating evidence, and Therrien had the restraint not to push it past that.

"You drove thirteen hundred miles to Boston in approximately twenty-four hours to meet your fiancée, and yet you picked up a hitchhiker with the intention of having a liaison with her at a motel?" Connor asked him.

"That is correct, sir," Therrien said.

In his closing statement, Alch made Therrien's story sound at least conceivable. But the story required the jury to assume, among other things, that both Oi and O'Donnell, the West Point captain and the decent-looking policeman, had erupted into irrational violence. The jury had to believe O'Donnell or Therrien, Connor said. "One of them is a hero, one of them is a liar. One of them is a hero, and one of them is a crazed killer." The jury believed O'Donnell. After nine and a half hours of deliberation, Therrien was found guilty of first-degree murder in both the death of William Shee-han and the death of John Oi.

The prosecutors and detectives who had worked on the investigation had the strong belief that they had solved the crime but not the mystery. The prosecution, of course, is not required to prove motive — the insur-ance policy was offered merely as a possibility — and Connor seemed under no illusion that he had. "We can never get inside that man's mind and discover what the real reason was," he told the jury. Would a man really commit premeditated murder for the rather indirect benefit of acquiring two hundred thousand dollars for a corporation he owned one-quarter of? Would a man murder to remove a ceiling of fifteen thousand dollars on his salary? How much more than fifteen thousand dollars could someone expect to be paid for managing a Cantonese-Polynesian restaurant in Marietta, Georgia? Was there something in the early rumors about gambling and the mob? Was someone else involved? Was Therrien rather than Wing Chin the partner John Oi suspected? What motive would be strong enough to explain murder?

Whether the insurance was the reason for John Oi's death or not, it did make Chin Enterprises, Incorporated, a rather well-off little corporation. Months before Therrien was brought to trial, the insurance company paid the beneficiary of John Oi's insurance, with no argument. A windfall of two hundred thousand dollars to an eighty-thousand-dollar corporation was, in a sense, the closest Armand Therrien had come to bettering himself in a big way. The corporation has problems, of course. It is the defendant in a civil suit filed by Cheryl Oi. Its vice-president is dead. Its secretary-treasurer has just begun serving two consecutive life terms at the Massachusetts Correctional Institution at Walpole.

Melisha Morganna Gibson

Cleveland, Tennessee
January 1977

RONNIE MADDUX met Wanda Gibson eight years ago, when she was a widow in her late twenties with three children and a lot of men visitors. They met in Cleveland, Tennessee, on the southeast side of town — a neighborhood that attracts some poor-white country people, who wander into Cleveland from the hill counties to work in a furniture factory, and some locals like Ronnie Maddux who never seem to work very long anywhere. "During the first two years, we went together on a regular basis," Maddux said later, in a statement to the Bradley County Sheriff's Department. "I quit going over to see her because of the drunks that hung around over there and because Joe Pete Cochran came over to where Wanda was living on Woolen Street looking for me with a sawed-off shotgun because of a gambling debt. Joe Pete Cochran cheated me out of the title to my car in a dice game, and I had to give him my title, my tags, and my keys. I had another set of keys, so I got Ronnie Goins to get the car and bring it to the corner where I was so I could go home. That was another reason I stayed away from Wanda. We didn't see each other for about eight months. We got back together just before she had Thomas Glenn Maddux, my son. He was born on the tenth day of March, 1970. We were together that time for about a year. Then I got married to Josephine Holder. I lived with her for about three months, then left when I found out she was pregnant when I married her. We got a divorce later. During this time, Wanda got pregnant with Melisha Morganna Gibson by Ronnie Fairbanks. Wanda and I were together again when Melisha was born. I knew when she was born that she belonged to Ronnie Fairbanks." A social worker who had reason to visit the home after the baby was born, in the spring of 1972, has described it as "one drunken party after another." A church worker also visited regularly, bringing clothing for the children and testimonies to the advantages of a Christian life. "Jesus loves everybody," the church worker said recently, "but those people didn't respond real well." The family called the new baby Ganna. When she was eleven months old, Ronnie Maddux and Wanda Gibson were indicted for beating her up. During the court proceedings, Ronnie and Wanda — inspired, some people in Cleveland suspect, less by ardor than by the rule protecting a wife from having to testify against her husband — became man and wife. And that is how Ronnie Maddux became Melisha Morganna Gibson's stepfather.

The doctor who treated Melisha at eleven months — treated her for a black eye and bruises of the back, thighs, chest, and face — was a pediatrician named

John Appling, who for ten years had been trying to persuade people in Cleveland that more had to be done to prevent child abuse. At his instigation, the Jaycees had raised enough money to construct a Child Shelter for temporary care, and a district child-care committee had been established. Before Appling had gone far in his crusade, though, it was clear that many people in town would have been happier if he confined himself to the quiet practice of pediatrics. Cleveland, its boosters often point out to visitors, is not some backward village in the southeast Tennessee hills but a steadily growing city with the advantages of diversified industry and a location right on the Interstate, between Chattanooga and Knoxville. Appling and others have argued that the very jobs Cleveland is so proud of generating are bound to attract the sort of displaced workers who, lacking the support of family and friends they had at home, may turn on their children from the stress of the first layoff. But Cleveland people tired quickly of being told that they lived in a center of child abuse. Cleveland has always been a place strongly bound to fundamentalist Christianity — a place where Baptists are likely to be found in church on Wednesday evenings as well as on Sunday mornings, a place that serves as international headquarters for two large Pentecostal denominations, a place that has grown from a town into a middle-sized city without allowing bars or even liquor stores. There was some feeling among Cleveland residents that the sort of incidents Appling kept haranguing them about could not happen in Cleveland — a feeling reinforced by the fact that the confidentiality imposed on the court handling child-abuse cases caused most of them to go unreported in the press.

Appling — a man who had treated hundreds of abused children like Melisha Gibson, a man who claimed that six to ten children in Bradley County died every year from child abuse — could not stop the harangue. He can talk about national studies and generally accepted theories on child abuse — about the special risks, for instance, faced by children of teen-age mothers and by illegitimate children and by children perceived by the family as being different in some way — but he tends to drift toward specific cases. When he discusses the details of a child-abuse case, he occasionally pauses to take a deep breath, as if willing himself under control. "I've gotten too emotional with it," Appling has said. "I see all these children in the emergency room beat all to hell, and then I see them *back* in the emergency room beat all to hell. The people seem like 'This child here is mine. He's my property. I can maim him. I can kill him. It's none of your business.'" People in the agency officially responsible for processing child-abuse cases in Bradley County — an agency recently renamed Human Services, but still referred to by just about everybody as Welfare — considered Dr. Appling an interfering zealot whose method of protecting children was to keep them away from their parents forever. The policy of the state happened to have the opposite emphasis — reuniting the family whenever possible. Once, a welfare-department county manager reacted to Appling's refusal to discharge a child from the hospital without additional reports on the child's home by threatening to have him arrested for kidnapping.

There was no question of releasing Melisha to the care of Ronnie Maddux and Wanda Gibson, who were then awaiting trial for beating her up. When she was discharged from the hospital, a welfare worker took her to a foster family; when that family moved away three months later, the worker placed Melisha in foster care with Mr. and Mrs. Gilbert Hawkins, who live on thirty acres at the end of a country road seven miles south of Cleveland. Gilbert Hawkins, who works at maintenance in a chemical plant near Cleveland, built his own house a few years ago, with the help of a nephew — a solid brick ranch house that looks as if it has never missed a day's cleaning. The Hawkinses, both of whom grew up in the country within a couple of miles of where they live now, are active members of the Goodwill Baptist Church. Mrs. Hawkins has known Ronnie Maddux's sister for years, but she tends to speak of Ronnie and Wanda Maddux as if they belonged to a different race of beings. "They just don't think like we do," she said not long ago. Mrs. Hawkins sometimes uses "love" as a synonym for "hug," so she can say that when foster babies are in the house it is not unusual for even her eighteen-year-old son to "pick them up and love them." The Hawkins family loved Melisha in both of the ways they use the word. They called her Missy. She grew into a lovely-looking blond little girl — shy with strangers but apparently talkative at home. She was subject to high fevers but otherwise healthy — an agile child who loved to do acrobatics. She lived as part of the Hawkins family for nearly three years — until it came time, last May, to return her to Ronnie and Wanda Maddux.

The Madduxes had been sentenced to what people in Tennessee call eleven twenty-nine — eleven months and twenty-nine days in the county jail, the maximum sentence for a misdemeanor. After some delay for appeal, they served six months. When they were released, in November of 1974, they settled down to what their social worker saw as a considerably more stable and sober life than they had led before. They eventually rented a tiny house, planted a vegetable garden, and even made a pass at sprucing the place up. They got by mostly on the Social Security payments Wanda Maddux drew as the beneficiary of her first husband. Apparently, Maddux hoped to make a big killing from a lawsuit in which he claimed to have suffered a back injury from falling down some stairs. A woman who lived across the street, Mattie Sue Riggs, said not long ago, "He'd say, 'Now, Mattie, anyone comes around here asking about me lifting anything heavy, don't you go talking to them.' And I said, 'Ronnie, I've not never seen you lift nothing no heavier than a dinner plate.' "

The Madduxes wanted the children back. By last February, the four older children had been returned — at different times, according to the normal welfare-department procedure. The children seemed content and reasonably well cared for, but the social worker, Judy Hampton, was still concerned about returning Melisha — the one child who was known to have been abused. Maddux had denied from the start that he and his wife had beaten Melisha; he even wrote a letter to the local paper denying it publicly. Still, Mrs. Hampton tried to talk Wanda Maddux into putting Melisha up for adoption. She refused. Mrs. Hampton waited until the end of the school year, on the theory that the presence of the older children at home would be a safety factor for Melisha. Then, with the consent of the juvenile court, she took Melisha back to her family.

There was nothing at all unusual about taking an abused child back to the family that had abused her. One alternative — legally terminating parental rights so that the child can be put up for adoption — is difficult practically to the point of impossibility under Tennessee law. Even children who have been beaten up are often eager to return to their own families, and their parents are often eager to have them back — an eagerness that may be affected in some cases by the fact that Aid to Families with Dependent Children payments represent the only form of welfare money available in southeast Tennessee. In the welfare department, there was a natural bureaucratic pressure to close cases and get children out of temporary foster homes. In theory, an interagency Child Protection Team that was organized a year ago in Cleveland by

David Sweitzer, the regional coördinator from the state Office of Child Development, was available for consultation about how to approach any child-abuse case, but the welfare department regarded the Child Protection Team mainly as a vehicle for Dr. Appling's interference. Routinely, a welfare worker — often overburdened with cases and paperwork, almost never having had any significant training in child protection — would recommend that a child be sent back home, the recommendation would be approved by the welfare department's chain of command, and the juvenile-court judge would order the child sent home. The judge's assent to the welfare report was considered so automatic in Bradley County that some foster parents who had become concerned about sending children back to homes they considered unsafe approached a local legislator last summer to ask whether it would be possible to have the judge impeached.

The Hawkinses were not among the protesting foster parents, but they were concerned all last summer about Missy. On trips to Cleveland, they found themselves detouring through the Madduxes' neighborhood to catch glimpses of her playing in the front yard. Finally, in the fall, Mrs. Hawkins called Ronnie Maddux's sister to ask if Missy could use a winter coat. The Madduxes relayed an invitation to bring the coat by, and, stretching the rules about visiting former foster children, the Hawkinses accepted. They were greeted cordially. Mrs. Hawkins took Missy's measurements so she could make her some dresses. Mr. Hawkins, who had been uneasy about the visit, could sense nothing amiss. Even Mrs. Hawkins had difficulty putting her finger on any specific indication that Missy was not well cared for — although she said later that when she was about to leave "Missy looked up with those beautiful brown eyes and said, 'Mommy, can I go back out to your house?' "

On her regular visits, Mrs. Hampton often found Missy being fussed over by her older sisters. The neighbors considered the Maddux family pleasant enough, although Ronnie Maddux seemed strict with the children about such matters as returning promptly from errands. He also had a tendency to let out a prolonged howl occasionally for no apparent reason. "Like none-none talk or people speaking tongues," Mattie Riggs has said. "I'd say, 'My Lord, Ronnie, you crazy?' And he'd say, 'I must be, Mattie.' "

On the night of October 11th, about four weeks after the Hawkinses' visit, Ronnie Maddux got angry at Melisha. Apparently, the trouble started when she would not go to sleep, and was aggravated when, in the early hours of the morning, she wet herself. On the morning of the twelfth, Maddux began making Melisha walk back and forth between the kitchen and an organ stool in the bedroom. "I wanted to tire her out so she would sleep," he explained later. "I got some hot sauce and made her take a tablespoon of it. She threw it up on the floor. . . . She began to slow down, so I told her to get on her toes and trot. A while later, I gave her another tablespoon of hot sauce, and she threw up again. . . . I was drinking whiskey. I made her keep walking back and forth all day to try to tire her out so she would sleep that night. . . . She asked me for a drink of water. I got a glass of water and told her if she would take the tablespoon of hot sauce I would give her a drink. She swallowed the hot sauce and I drank the glass of water." Maddux said he continued to make Melisha walk back and forth after supper, hitting her with a stick as she passed him. That night, he got her up and put her in a cold shower, apparently because she had wet her mattress. On the morning of the thirteenth, when he tried to wake her up she didn't respond. He began to rub her with alcohol, trying to bring her around.

That morning, Mrs. Hawkins was hemming some corduroy pants she had made for Missy when the telephone rang. It was her sister-in-law, saying, "There's something wrong down at Missy's house." A moment later, the doorbell rang. "It was two of my welfare workers," Mrs. Hawkins said later. "I knew the minute I saw them. 'Did he beat her up again?' I said. They said, 'Mrs. Hawkins, it's worse than that this time.'" Melisha had never awakened. The next day, Ronnie and Wanda Maddux were charged with first-degree murder, and held without bail.

Investigations were launched. Committees were formed. The state Commissioner of Human Services disciplined three members of the Bradley County office, and almost everybody else in the office joined in a one-day walkout in protest — arguing, rather persuasively, that the workers involved were being scapegoated after handling the case more or less the way it would have been handled by any welfare worker who followed normal state procedures. The commissioner announced a moratorium on returning abused children to their families, and speculated on the possibility of easing the procedures available for terminating parental rights. Members of a Teamsters local picketed the Governor's Mansion, urging that Ronnie and Wanda Maddux be given the death penalty if found guilty. Hank Snow, the country-music singer, wrote the governor, "I've heard countless people say that if these radicals were burned in the electric chair or even lynched in the city square, it would start some of these lowdowns to giving some serious thought before committing these gruesome crimes." There was some talk about sterilization as a way to prevent child-abusers from producing more children to abuse. Those in the child-protection field who believe that reform should concentrate on prevention of child abuse rather than on punishment of abusers found themselves grateful that the state legislature will not be in session until spring.

In Cleveland, a thousand people attended Melisha's funeral. The Sheriff's Department decided it would be prudent to hold the Madduxes in a jail outside the county — presumably not the state penitentiary, where Melisha's natural father is serving time for armed robbery. Welfare workers complained of harassment and even threats. There are people in Cleveland who believe that the intensity of reaction there can be traced to some acceptance of guilt for not having heeded the warnings of Dr. Appling long ago. Appling and David Sweitzer, who blame Melisha's death partly on rigidity and secrecy in the welfare department, used the public outcry to exert pressure for interagency coöperation and improved training, although in one of his first meetings with the Human Services commissioner Appling found himself unable to get away from the subject of three children who had been returned that day to a home he considered potentially unsafe. Appling and Sweitzer finally won agreement that every child-abuse case in the county would be referred to the Child Protection Team — a team that now includes not only a psychiatrist and a pediatrician and a social worker but an attorney to represent the child's interests in court. The public outcry had a different meaning for the forces fighting a referendum in the November election which would have permitted liquor stores in Bradley County: they pointed to Ronnie Maddux's behavior as an example of what drink could lead to, and they defeated the referendum easily. Hank Snow came to Cleveland for a concert to benefit the fund that local people are raising to enlarge the Child Shelter, which has been renamed the Melisha Gibson Child Shelter.

Family Problems

Manchester, New Hampshire
July 1978

HANK PIASECNY, like a lot of people in Manchester, worked his way up from the mills. The banks of the Merrimack River, which cuts right through Manchester, are still lined with the massive old red brick buildings that once drew people like Hank Piasecny's parents from Poland and his wife's parents from French Quebec and thousands of other people from Ireland or from the rocky farms of upper New England. The buildings on the banks of the Merrimack were once filled with shoe factories and foundries and the Amoskeag Mills — a textile operation that employed more than twenty thousand people before it went under in the thirties. Hank Piasecny, one of seven children of a shoe-factory worker, started working in a shoe factory himself at fourteen. When he came home from the Second World War, he opened a corner grocery store, and then a filling station that later branched out into hunting and fishing equipment. He was a hard worker, and he was fortunate enough to acquire the New England distributorship for Arkansas Traveler boats at about the time the aluminum-boat market was beginning to expand. By the early sixties, he was the proprietor of a thriving sporting-goods store called Hank's Sport Center. He sponsored a Golden Gloves team that included his own son, Terry, as one of its stars. He had an attractive wife and a teenage daughter who seemed to be talented at anything she turned to. He often joined his customers on deer-hunting trips, and people who discussed his skill as a hunter sometimes said, "Where he goes, the deer follow." In the southern part of New Hampshire, public officials who were also outdoorsmen were likely to be friends of Hank Piasecny. He was an outgoing, rough-talking man — known to have a temper that could transform rough talk suddenly into violence. "He'd give you any damn thing he had," a close friend of Piasecny during that period has said. "But he didn't mind having a fight — I'll tell you."

One person Piasecny didn't mind fighting with was his wife, Doris. Apparently, the Piasecny marriage was violent from the beginning. Doris Piasecny, who worked as a secretary in downtown Manchester, had grown up in a miserable river-bottom neighborhood known as Skeag Village. She had a longing for material objects that strained Piasecny's income and his temper. At one time, the family owned three Cadillacs. Hank Piasecny was ferociously jealous. He drank a lot. His wife took a lot of pills. Terry Piasecny remembers from childhood that when his father's spirits were high — particularly in a hunting camp in the St. John River valley, in Maine — "you could really be on the top of the world with him." More often, his spirits were low. Arguments between him and Doris would build up to the point at which their daughter, Susan, suddenly burst out of the house to call for help. The Manchester police came out regularly to calm Piasecny down. At least once, he was convicted of assaulting his wife. "I used to hope that one of them would die," Susan Piasecny said later. "So it would all end."

In 1963, after some separations and some false starts toward divorce and some contempt citations against Piasecny for violating a court order barring him from the house, Doris Piasecny was finally granted a divorce. She got the house and most of the possessions. He set up housekeeping in the back of Hank's Sport Center. Terry, who had married young, had been away from home for some time. Susan was in her second year at Colby College. Although Hank Piasecny had seemed unwilling to accept the divorce, he and his wife seemed to get along better divorced than married. She even went out with him occasionally. She also went out with other people. One night, around Christmas of 1963, she invited some people who had been drinking at a bar called the Venice Room back to the house for a nightcap. Among them was a bachelor named John Betley — a prominent Manchester architect, who, after leaving his house late that evening to garage his car, had decided to drop in to the Venice Room for a drink. Eventually, the gathering at Doris Piasecny's house began to break up. John Betley and Doris Piasecny were left alone in the house. Not long after that, according to the way the police later pieced together what must have happened, Hank Piasecny emerged from his hiding place, a kitchen knife in his hand, and killed both his wife and John Betley. Doris Piasecny was stabbed eleven times. John Betley was stabbed thirteen times.

In New Hampshire the legal definition of insanity is rather broad. To accept a plea of not guilty by reason of insanity, a judge or jury need not be persuaded that the defendant was unable to distinguish between right and wrong but merely that his crime was the product of mental illness. A couple of hours after the murders, Hank Piasecny was found in the back of Hank's Sport Center, having smashed his truck into a turnpike guardrail nearby. He was drunk and raving and holding a deer rifle that he managed to fire once before passing out. He was later examined by a prominent Boston psychiatrist hired by the defense. He was examined by psychiatrists acting for the state. It was agreed that Hank Piasecny was legally insane — a paranoid schizophrenic. "Mr. Piasecny has always been a rather seriously disturbed person with masochistic, passive, dependent, narcissistic trends," one of the state's psychiatrists said. "Often he has very effectively repressed realities which were incompatible with his deep need to be recognized as a real man by his wife and a substantial person by the community."

The state accepted Hank Piasecny's plea, and he was committed to the New Hampshire Hospital at Concord

— "for life until or unless earlier discharged, released or transferred by due course of law." The state attorney general's office, which handles all murder prosecutions in New Hampshire, could argue that, the state's own psychiatrists having found Piasecny insane, bringing him to trial instead of accepting the plea would have been fruitless. The suspicion lingered in Manchester, though, that Piasecny had escaped the penitentiary or the electric chair for reasons having nothing to do with psychiatry. Rumors had circulated about the murders from the beginning. Although John Betley and Doris Piasecny were found fully clothed, there were people in Manchester who insisted the bodies were nude and mutilated. It was said that the party at Doris Piasecny's that night had included an important judge, or perhaps more than one judge. It was said that Hank Piasecny's plea of insanity had been accepted because of a coverup, or because of influence exerted by some of his old hunting buddies. There were a lot of people in Manchester who thought that Hank Piasecny had managed to get away with murder.

After spending a year in a maximum-security section of the hospital, Piasecny settled into a relatively comfortable life in Concord. His brothers and sister, who were trying to maintain his shop for him, visited regularly. Terry brought the grandchildren. Piasecny's children had apparently chosen to believe that he had no idea what he was doing when he stabbed their mother and John Betley; some of his brothers had apparently chosen to believe that he may not have committed the crime at all. The hospital has a pitch-

and-putt golf course, and Piasecny spent a lot of time on it. Except for some problems early in his stay with an inmate named John McGrath, who had been committed after killing several members of his own family, Piasecny seemed to have adjusted relatively well to institutional life. Two years after he was committed, his lawyer petitioned for his release, arguing that he was no longer a danger to himself or others.

One of the state-hospital psychiatrists had some reservations about approving the release. His report said, "I cannot in all good conscience in any way state that the patient represents no further risk to the community whatsoever." In general, though, the psychiatrists agreed that Hank Piasecny, surely insane at the time of the murders, had recovered to the point of being able to live in his own community with the aid of some regular psychiatric care. The state attorney general's office opposed even a gradual release. John Betley's sister wrote the judge in the case a bitter letter, hinting that Piasecny had been protected from the start and expressing outrage that the court could sanction the release of "such an evil person." When the release was indeed sanctioned, the attorney general appealed to the state supreme court — unsuccessfully. On August 6, 1966, two and a half years after he was arrested for killing his wife and John Betley, Hank Piasecny returned to Manchester, a free man.

The life Piasecny settled into seemed to be calmer than the one he had left. After a couple of years, an entrance for the interstate sliced through the property of Hank's Sport Center, and Piasecny did not attempt to find a new location. He went to work for the boat store run by Arthur Pellenz, a friendly competitor from earlier times. The three-Cadillac days were over for Piasecny, but he seemed to get by with a simpler life. When Terry moved his family to a small house on a river an hour north of Manchester, Hank Piasecny became a regular Sunday visitor — fly-fishing in the river, taking Terry's eldest son into the woods for his first buck in the same way he had taken Terry. Even without three Cadillacs, he was still a man who might show up at the wake of a prominent citizen, and at Pellenz's boat store he was still a man who spoke bluntly. But "peaceful" was a word sometimes used about the life Piasecny led in Manchester — except when it came to his relationship with his daughter.

It is often said in Manchester that Susan Piasecny was a talented and remarkably intelligent girl who simply never recovered from the shock of her mother's murder. In high school, she did seem to be the sort of daughter who would make any father proud — a fine-looking girl who seemed to have a natural gift for music and art and athletics and scholarship. She was an honor student. She was a good enough athlete to teach skiing and riding and golf. Even before that day in 1963 when the Colby dean met her after class to tell her there was trouble at home, though, there had been episodes that would have surprised anyone in Manchester who took Susan Piasecny to be a model of achievement. When she was fourteen, she arrived home hours late from a babysitting job and reported having been abducted — a story the police eventually decided she might have made up. When she was sixteen, she was taken to a hospital in Nashua, temporarily unable to speak. After her mother's death, she was a patient in a Massachusetts mental hospital for several weeks. She left Colby, and left another college after that. Still, she eventually finished college, got married, and, in the fall of 1967, entered the medical school of the University of Vermont.

After two starts, she withdrew from medical school for good. Her marriage was deteriorating. Depressions had forced her to seek help again at mental hospitals. Shortly after her marriage broke up, she was found unconscious in a small New Hampshire town, apparently having been beaten or tossed from a car. She implied that her husband had hired thugs to beat her up. The Manchester police were not convinced. The incident reminded them of the babysitting abduction. It also reminded them of the reports years before that a local golfer who had become involved with Susan when she was a teenager had been beaten up by friends of Hank Piasecny. In 1970, Susan Piasecny entered the New Hampshire Hospital at Concord, depressed and suicidal. She remained there for three years. Shortly after her release, she married a fellow patient named Edward Hughes. Shortly after that, it was reported that Edward Hughes had walked into the bathroom of their apartment, slit his throat with a Gillette razor blade, and walked back into the living room to die in the presence of his wife.

After her second husband's death, Susan Hughes

worked now and then at one nursing home or another, but her life seemed dominated by pills and bad checks and petty brushes with the law and fights with her father. They tried living together for a while — renting the small brick bungalow Terry had left when he moved away — but they finally had to split up. Living in the same house with his daughter, Hank Piasecny apparently started seeing in her the mannerisms that had angered him about his wife. In his anger, he may have sometimes called her Doris instead of Susan. After Susan moved out, there were periods when her father swore he wanted nothing more to do with her. She was regularly in trouble — forging prescriptions for pills or stealing from friends or bouncing checks. The girl who had once seemed capable of doing anything she chose to do was considered by her uncles and her aunts and even her own father a persistent disgrace to the Piasecny name. In June of 1977, Hank Piasecny and his daughter had a violent argument — he may have hit her or shoved her or shaken her — and he said he never wanted to see her or hear from her again.

On the Friday before last Labor Day weekend, Susan Hughes's name appeared in the court column of the *Manchester Union Leader*. The item said, "Sue E. Piasecny, 35, of 367 Hanover St., also known as Susan Hughes, entered no plea to two counts of forgery, both felony complaints." She telephoned the reporter responsible, demanding to know why he had included her maiden name — a mention, she said, that was likely to drive her father to distraction, or violence. That night, she told some friends visiting her apartment that she feared her father might kill her because of his belief that she had dragged the family name through the mud once again. She showed them a knife she intended to use to defend herself. She showed them newspaper clippings about her mother's murder.

Early the next morning — Saturday of Labor Day weekend — the police went to Hank Piasecny's house. Susan Hughes had phoned to say that her father was so distraught she was afraid he might harm himself. They found Piasecny lying face down in the hallway. Half of his head had been blown off. A shotgun was at his side. The headline in the next day's *Union Leader* said, "HENRY (HANK) PIASECNY SHOOTS HIMSELF DEAD." The lead-in headline said, "CHARGED IN '63 SLAYINGS." Most people in Manchester figured that the guilt had finally caught up with Hank Piasecny — that he hadn't got away with murder after all. One or two of his brothers were said to believe that Hank Piasecny's daughter had driven him to his death. Susan Hughes herself had another theory: she said her father had been murdered.

She did not stop at merely offering the theory. She called the county attorney. She hounded the police. She suggested some suspects — John McGrath, for instance, the murderer at the state hospital, who had escaped several years before. Once, she pounded on the door of the police chief's office, shouting that her father had been murdered but no one would do anything about it. The police were unimpressed. Susan Hughes, after all, had come in with some wild tales in the past. Finally, three and a half weeks after Hank Piasecny died, his daughter, claiming reasonable ground to suspect that he had met his death by unlawful means, petitioned the superior court for a warrant to have the body disinterred and an autopsy performed. The petition made a claim that Susan Hughes had often made to the police — that there was a second bullet hole in her father's body. "In the early morning of September 5, 1977," the petition said, "Susan E. Hughes went to the funeral home and examined the body of her father, observing a puncture wound in the left chest which she was able to probe to a depth of 2½ to 3 inches." The petition was granted. The autopsy was performed. A hole was found on the left side of Hank Piasecny's chest. A .22 slug was found in his body.

When photographs taken at the death scene were reëxamined, it turned out that the second bullet hole was not the only suspicious detail that had been overlooked. Although Piasecny's head wound would have killed him instantly, the body was at least ten feet away from the pool of blood. The gun was in an awkward position across the back of his right arm; the wound in his head was on the left instead of the right. It may be that the police quickly assumed that what they found was a suicide because that is what they were prepared to find. People in Manchester had been half expecting Hank Piasecny to commit suicide for years, after all, and those expectations had been brought to the surface by the phone call from Piasecny's daughter. The possibility of reëxamining the scene itself no longer existed by the time of the autopsy. The house had been cleaned. The police picked up one lead, though, during conversations at the autopsy: Susan Hughes, it turned out, had told the county attorney and a few other people about the second wound the day after the murder, before her trip to the funeral home. It was true that she had been at the death scene shortly after Piasecny's body was discovered, but the police who were there agreed on one detail: the body was covered, and Susan Hughes had no opportunity to examine it.

A month passed before Susan Hughes admitted having shot her father — shot him first in the chest with a .22 she had stolen from her cousin, and then in the head with his own shotgun. A lot of theories were offered in Manchester as to why, having got away with it, she instigated an investigation that would lead to her arrest. There was a theory that she could collect Hank Piasecny's insurance only if he died by means other than suicide. In fact, Piasecny had very little life insurance, and its beneficiary was Terry. A lot of people thought, of course, that Susan Hughes simply wanted to be punished and had found herself frustrated by the police department's acceptance of a patently sloppy attempt to give the shooting the appearance of a suicide. Some people believed that her real interest was in showing up the police of Manchester — her adversaries for years — or in defiantly dragging the Piasecny name through the mud for the benefit of her uncles and aunts. There were those who thought Susan Hughes might have just wanted attention.

She was examined several times by psychiatrists. A psychiatrist for the state — the same psychiatrist who had been in charge of examining Piasecny for the state in 1964 — said she was "suffering from a schizophrenic reaction of the chronic undifferentiated type." It was the same diagnosis he had offered for her father; he testified, in fact, that the trouble might have been inherited. The assistant attorney general in the case, Peter Heed, is normally reluctant to accept pleas of not guilty by reason of insanity. Because of a recent New Hampshire Supreme Court decision, the state can be required to prove beyond a reasonable doubt every two years that an inmate of the state hospital would be a danger to himself or others if released. That burden of proof being almost impossible to meet in the case of anyone who has behaved reasonably well at the hospital, a defendant who is committed for life is more likely to remain committed for two years. Heed did, though, decide to accept a plea of not guilty by reason of insanity from Susan Hughes. It was not the psychiatric reports that persuaded him. In a recent murder case that Heed tried, all four psychiatrists who took the stand had testified that the defendant was insane, and the jury had found him sane — and guilty. Heed says he accepted Susan Hughes's plea because he believes her to be insane, and believes that any juror would find her insane no matter what psychiatrists testified. "She had committed the perfect crime," he said recently. "Her very own action led to her arrest. Susan Hughes was the first person I've dealt with who really comes under what the insanity defense was meant to encompass." Susan Hughes was sent to the New Hampshire Hospital — "for life until or unless earlier discharged, released or transferred by due process of law."

The verdict did not cause the grumbling that had taken place when Hank Piasecny was sent to the state hospital, but there are, of course, people in Manchester who do not believe Susan Hughes is insane. Some of her uncles apparently believe her to be simply evil. Some members of Edward Hughes's family are now wondering out loud whether Hughes committed suicide after all. A former member of the attorney general's office who did not believe Hank Piasecny's plea should have been accepted seems to feel the same way about Susan Hughes's plea. "Of course she wanted to get caught," he said recently. "But that's not insanity — that's a sense of guilt. A lot of murders get solved that way."

In the two months between her father's death and her confession, Susan Hughes had seemed more and more insane to the people observing her — distraught, obsessive, sometimes hysterical. Once, she went to the police station to show detectives some graffiti she said someone had printed on her car in lipstick — a warning that she would be the next victim. For a while, most of her energies seemed to be taken up with an attempt to persuade an acquaintance to confess the murder. Now she seems rational and intelligent, sitting in a dayroom at the New Hampshire Hospital — a large room with green linoleum floors and color pictures cut from magazines on the wall and the sounds of afternoon television and desultory Ping-Pong broken now and then by some patient's sudden outburst. Discussing the death of her father with a visitor not long ago, she said she had shot him in self-defense, then shot him again with his own shotgun for seemingly contradictory reasons that didn't seem contradictory in the shock of it all — to put him out of pain if he was still alive, perhaps, or to make certain he wouldn't recover and kill her. "If I had really wanted to make it look like a suicide," she said, "I would have rolled him over and shot him in the chest to obliterate the hole." She said she had insisted on the murder investigation because she believed the family — Terry's family — would prefer to think that Hank Piasecny died a murder victim rather than a suicide. She said she had not believed that the investigation would lead to her arrest. She talked about growing up as the daughter of Hank and Doris Piasecny — about being boarded out during the week as a child while both parents were working, about hearing the arguments start to build and knowing she would have to run for help, about discussions during the last year of Doris Piasecny's life as to whether or not her husband would kill her. "I've talked about all the bad things," she said at the door, as the visitor waited for the attendant to bring the key. "But there was love, too."

Todo Se Paga

Riverside, California
February 1979

THE FEUD between the Ahumadas and the Lozanos, everyone agrees, began late one night in January of 1964, when John Ahumada, Sr., was beaten so badly that slivers of his skull were driven into his brain. It happened in Casa Blanca. Technically, Casa Blanca is a section of Riverside, California, a county seat sixty miles east of Los Angeles; spiritually, Casa Blanca is unto itself. Before the Second World War, when Riverside was still a quiet trading center for citrus growers, Casa Blanca had been isolated from the rest of the town for half a century — a square-mile patch cut out of acre upon acre of orange groves. Mexican farm workers who settled on the East Side of Riverside, close to downtown, gradually learned to deal with Anglos and blacks and the city authorities; Casa Blanca remained something close to a rural Mexican village. In 1949, it had only two paved streets. In the years after the war, the citrus-packing sheds where many Casa Blanca men had worked closed or burned down. A double-lane deposited a strip of automobile dealerships next to one corner of Casa Blanca. Over the objections of many Casa Blanca residents, the local grade school — "the Mexican consulate," one former resident calls it — was closed as part of a citywide integration plan. Eventually, rising real-estate prices and increased industry in Orange County, the sprawl southeast of Los Angeles, began to turn Riverside into a bedroom community for what had itself been a bedroom community — replacing the orange groves near one border of Casa Blanca with a middle-class housing development called Woodhaven. Still, Casa Blanca retained a feeling of being rural. Still, Casa Blanca remained unto itself — a place where uninvited strangers were challenged. Having never expected concern or justice from the outside, Casa Blanca remained a place that took care of its own territory and its own problems and its own feuds.

John Ahumada had been having some drinks with John Hernandez, whose wife was a Lozano. They had apparently been friendly enough in El Flamingo, where the drinking started, but some angry words were exchanged at the Casa Blanca Café, where they found themselves about one-thirty in the morning. Hernandez and Ahumada walked across the street to a parking lot next to the railroad tracks that form one boundary of Casa Blanca. They were joined eventually by two of Hernandez's brothers-in-law who lived nearby, Marcos and Roman Lozano — carrying tire irons, according to one account, or perhaps a part from a commercial ice-cream mixer. John Ahumada ended up in the hospital, on the critical list. Roman and Marcos

Lozano ended up in court, where, contrary to the Casa Blanca tradition of not coöperating with outside authorities, John Ahumada testified against them. They were sent to prison for assault with a deadly weapon. Although everyone agrees that the fight across from the Casa Blanca Café was the beginning of the feud, it is not clear which family was left with a wrong to avenge. Was it the Ahumadas, one of whom had been beaten so savagely that his arm was partly paralyzed and his speech remained slurred? Or was it the Lozanos, two of whom served time in state prison because an Ahumada had broken the code that required Casa Blanca people to settle their arguments in Casa Blanca?

For twelve years after Roman and Marcos Lozano were sent to state prison, there were no incidents between the Lozanos and the Ahumadas violent enough to come to the attention of the police. In Casa Blanca, the explanation normally offered for that hiatus is simple: the next generation of Lozanos and Ahumadas, children at the time of the fight across from the bar, needed a dozen years to grow old enough to kill each other. In the meantime, there were some schoolyard fistfights. Apparently, Johnny Lozano Hernandez would tell Johnny Ahumada that his father was a snitch, and a fight would start. Words would pass between Richard Lozano and Danny Ahumada, Johnny's younger brother, and another fight would start. "The seeds were there," someone who knew both families said recently. "All they had to do was scrape the earth a little bit."

In those years, the most ferocious battles engaged in by the young men of Casa Blanca pitted them against the young men of some other *barrio* rather than against each other — Casa Blanca fighting people from the East Side who had dared to drive into the neighborhood in force, Casa Blanca fighting a crowd from Corona or Rubidoux because someone had stared too long at a Casa Blanca girl. When Casa Blanca was not fighting another *barrio,* it was often fighting the police.

There were a few years, beginning in the late sixties, when almost any Mexican *barrio* in southern California was dangerous territory for Anglo police. For those years, when confrontation was part of what seemed to be a unified movement for the betterment of La Raza, gang members were transformed into Brown Berets, street toughs began thinking of themselves as Chicano militants, and juvenile offenders learned to refer to the rest of the world as "the Anglo-dominant society" instead of "paddies." In the words of one former Casa Blanca Brown Beret, "We were rebels without a cause who became rebels with a cause."

Even when the movement evaporated, though, hostility toward the police remained in Casa Blanca, fed by the hostility toward outsiders which had existed for decades. Riverside police cruisers were able to drive peacefully through the Mexican or black neighborhoods of the East Side, but a policeman driving into Casa Blanca at night could consider himself fortunate to be met by a beer bottle instead of a rifle shot. One night in August of 1975, in a cornfield on the edge of Casa

Blanca, sniping and harassment broke into what amounted to open warfare. Five people were wounded. Two young men from Casa Blanca — Danny Ahumada and Larry Romero, a member of a family close to the Ahumadas — were arrested for shooting at a police officer. "Casa Blanca had a reputation for sticking together," a young man who grew up fighting there said not long ago. "Even if we had problems, we'd never think of killing each other."

They started killing each other on Christmas, 1976. Richard Lozano and a cousin who was visiting from Arizona, Gilbert Lozano Sanchez, were shot at from a passing car. Lozano was not hit; Sanchez was killed. By the spring of 1978, when James Richardson, a young courthouse reporter for the *Riverside Press-Enterprise,* pieced together court and police records to construct a chronology of the violence that the Lozanos and the Ahumadas had visited upon each other, three people had been killed, two people had been crippled, and any number of people had been sideswiped or shot at. Richard Lozano has been killed since then. Most of the shootings have been carried out with a sudden, dramatic ferocity. Danny Ahumada was grabbed by the hair and shot twice in the head point-blank with a .22-calibre pistol — an attack he somehow survived, although he was even more seriously disabled than his father. Johnny Lozano Hernandez was shot down before a dozen witnesses after a dispute during which, according to Johnny Ahumada, "he began to tell me my brother was a snitch, my brother was a dog." Ruben (Redeye) Romero — who, along with Johnny Ahumada, had been tried but acquitted in Johnny Hernandez's death — was killed at a Casa Blanca filling station by three young gunmen who shot him, knelt at his body, crossed themselves, and shot him again at point-blank range. When Richard Lozano was killed, seven weeks later, his uncle Raul Lozano, who had been tried but not convicted in the shooting of Danny Ahumada, was seen smearing the blood of his fallen nephew on his hand and tasting it, presumably as a symbol of vengeance owed.

The feud between the Lozanos and the Ahumadas lacks symmetry. There are family members who are not involved. John Lozano, the father of the recently murdered Richard, claims that he still has a friendly hello for John Ahumada, Sr., when they meet in Casa Blanca. Even those who are involved seem to go along for weeks, or even months, without retaliation. Most of the encounters that end in death or serious injury seem mere chance — a moment when someone is caught alone or when someone makes an insulting remark. "They're in no hurry," a man familiar with Mexican-American neighborhoods in southern California explained not long ago. "In the *barrio,* people say, '*Todo se paga.*'" Everything is paid.

In the *barrio,* the brutal simplicity ordinarily associated with a blood feud — an eye for an eye — is complicated by the element of pride. "You killed my brother, so I will kill your brother" sometimes seems to become "You killed my brother and that makes you think you are stronger than we are and can look down on us, so, to show that's not true, I will kill your brother." When Roman Lozano was asked recently why the feud had started again in 1976, he said, "They knew their dad was a snitch, and they had an uncle who was a homosexual. They had to prove that they were manly." People on both sides have complained of having their houses fired on from passing cars, but they complain even more bitterly of having carloads of their enemies drive by and throw kisses as a gesture of contempt. One of Johnny Ahumada's theories about the origin of the seventies violence is that the Lozanos were jealous because only Danny Ahumada and Larry Romero were singled out after the 1975 cornfield melee for having shot at the police. "They want to prove their heart," Johnny says. "They don't want to lose their pride. That's what makes them revengeful."

There are people in Riverside who believe that the violence between the Ahumadas and the Lozanos no longer has anything to do with the 1964 assault. "It's not like the Hatfields and the McCoys," a man who grew up in Casa Blanca said recently. "The underlying motive is drugs." Marcos and John Lozano have both been convicted on serious heroin charges at one time or another. There are people in Riverside who say that some of the younger Ahumadas — or their allies, the Romeros — may have pushed into Lozano drug-dealing territory while the Lozanos were in prison. There are people in Riverside who say that the argument between the two families is actually an argument between the two Mexican prison gangs that have emerged in California in the past several years — the Mexican Mafia and Nuestra Familia — one of which is supposedly challenging the other over control of drugs in Casa Blanca.

In the *barrio*, it is common to hear drugs offered as an underlying motive for any excess in violence or wealth. Members of the vice-and-narcotics squad in Riverside tend not to be believers in the drug-war theory. Redeye Romero, who is sometimes described as a "hard-core biker," was, like a lot of hard-core bikers, suspected of being a bagman in the heroin trade, but he was not thought to be in a position to challenge anybody for control of serious drug traffic. The only drug charge ever brought against an Ahumada was made when Danny was shot: the policemen who took charge of his clothing reported finding twelve balloons of heroin in the trousers. An investigator for the Riverside County district attorney's office who serves on a state task force dealing with prison gangs says that neither gang had anything to do with the shootings in Casa Blanca or control of the drug traffic in Casa Blanca. He says, in fact, that Nuestra Familia conducted its own investigation to make certain that the death of Johnny Lozano Hernandez, apparently a Nuestra Familia member, had been strictly a private affair. "If it's true," a Casa Blanca native said recently of the theory that competing gangs are involved, "it's just one more reason for hating each other."

Mary Ahumada, the wife of the original victim, sometimes speaks of the Ahumadas as respectable citizens who have somehow found themselves locked in a feud with criminals. When she was informed recently that her son Danny might be sent to state prison for having been caught with a stolen pistol while on probation for the drug charge and an old auto-theft conviction, she said, "My boys were never mixed up in that sort of thing." It is true that the Ahumadas have not served time in state prison, although they are familiar with the Riverside County jail. Mrs. Ahumada is a handsome, loquacious woman who, as Sister Mary, runs a small evangelical congregation that specializes in teenagers who have strayed from the Lord's path. The Lozanos sometimes speak of her as a hypocritical Holy Roller who goads her sons to violence. "People tend to pull you down," she says. " 'Why doesn't she save her own sons? Why doesn't she save *their* souls?' Yes, I've had remarks from police officers in the past that have been cruel." (Sister Mary's ministry has not been completely without effect on her sons: Johnny wore a gold cross in his lapel throughout his trial for the murder of Johnny Hernandez.) Although the Ahumadas' ally Redeye Romero was known as a hard-core biker, he was also known as one of the founders of the Brown Berets in Casa Blanca — someone who showed up at meetings now and then as a spokesman for *barrio* youth. When he was killed, he was referred to in the press as a "street leader," although he was about to go to prison for an armed-robbery conviction. Policemen in Riverside are unimpressed by the prominence of the Ahumadas and the Romeros. In fact, to some policemen, particularly Anglo policemen who are not overly concerned about the effects of heroin on Mexicans in a remote *barrio,* serious drug dealers have the advantage over street leaders of trying to avoid incidents that only attract the authorities to their place of business — incidents like firing on police cruisers.

Some people in Casa Blanca believe that the Riverside police are not saddened by the sight of Ahumadas and Lozanos killing and maiming each other. The police have in fact made a lot of arrests in the shootings, but the closest thing to a conviction has been Raul Lozano pleading *nolo contendere* to a charge of having been an accessory to the shooting of Danny Ahumada. When Georgie Ahumada, the younger brother of Johnny and Danny, was released without charge after having been picked up for the murder of Richard Lozano, Mary Ahumada said she had told Georgie to trust in God, but most people charged with one of the shootings have trusted in the lack of witnesses willing to testify. After Georgie Ahumada went free, the deputy district attorney who has handled all of the feud shootings said, "This is the usual situation where twenty people see the killing and all of them say, 'I didn't see it.'" Even two of Richard Lozano's uncles who were present when he was killed declined to coöperate with the authorities. Richard's father, John Lozano, does not seem upset that his brothers would not help to bring his son's killer to justice. "They're the type that don't like to testify," he says.

Some people in Casa Blanca who are not related to either family have been unable to stay out of the feud.

People who witnessed shootings have had their houses fired upon, making it necessary, in some cases, for their own young men to prove that they cannot be treated as weaklings. One of the young men who is awaiting trial for the murder of Redeye Romero seems to have got involved originally because his mother became friendly with Johnny Lozano Hernandez's mother upon moving into the neighborhood. ("They were the only ones who treated us with respect," he says.) A young man named William DeHaro, who was shot to death last September, may have been killed simply because he remained friendly with the Lozanos after a warning to avoid them. Some people in Casa Blanca — particularly older people — seem to be able to stay out of the feud. "You don't dare choose sides," one of them has said. "You talk to both. You go to the funerals for both."

Many of the Lozanos and Ahumadas and Romeros have moved out of Casa Blanca in the last year or so, partly in an effort to sleep peacefully through the night, but they return constantly. Everyone remains well armed; when the police search the house of someone involved in the feud, they invariably come up with a small arsenal. Complaining recently about some people having shot at his house the previous evening, John Lozano mentioned that he had taken the precaution of borrowing a machine gun. The Ahumadas and the Lozanos both say they would like the feud to end, but no one is optimistic that it will. A new generation is gradually growing old enough to kill each other. "You can see it in the ten-year-olds," Johnny Ahumada said recently. "They look at you, and you can see their hatred." Standing in the hall of the Riverside County Courthouse not long ago, John Lozano, who had just entered a guilty plea to possession of heroin for sale, was equally pessimistic. "I wish it would end," he said. "I'm facing four years, and I'll be out of the picture — which, in a way, I'm glad."

It's Just Too Late

Knoxville, Tennessee
March 1979

UNTIL SHE WAS SIXTEEN, FaNee Cooper was what her parents sometimes called an ideal child. "You'd never have to correct her," FaNee's mother has said. In sixth grade, FaNee won a spelling contest. She played the piano and the flute. She seemed to believe what she heard every Sunday at the Beaver Dam Baptist Church about good and evil and the hereafter. FaNee was not an outgoing child. Even as a baby, she was uncomfortable when she was held and cuddled. She found it easy to tell her parents that she loved them but difficult to confide in them. Particularly compared to her sister, Kristy, a cheerful, open little girl two and a half years younger, she was reserved and introspective. The thoughts she kept to herself, though, were apparently happy thoughts. Her eighth-grade essay on Christmas — written in a remarkably neat hand — talked of the joys of helping put together toys for her little brother, Leo, Jr., and the importance of her parents' reminder that Christmas is the birthday of Jesus.

Her parents were the sort of people who might have
been expected to have an ideal child. As a boy, Leo
Cooper had been called "one of the greatest high-school
basketball players ever developed in Knox County." He
went on to play basketball at East Tennessee State, and
he married the homecoming queen, JoAnn Henson.
After college, Cooper became a high-school basketball
coach and teacher and, eventually, an administrator.
By the time FaNee turned thirteen, in 1973, he was in
his third year as the principal of Gresham Junior High
School, in Fountain City — a small Knox County town
that had been swallowed up by Knoxville when the suburbs began to move north. A tall man, with curly black
hair going on gray, Leo Cooper has an elaborate way
of talking ("Unless I'm very badly mistaken, he has
never related to me totally the content of his conversation") and a manner that may come from years of
trying to leave errant junior-high-school students with
the impression that a responsible adult is magnani-
mous, even humble, about invariably being in the right.
His wife, a high-school art teacher, paints and does
batik, and created the name FaNee because she liked
the way it looked and sounded — it sounds like
"Fawn-*ee*" when the Coopers say it — but the impression she gives is not of artiness but of soft-spoken
small-town gentility. When she found, in the course of
cleaning up FaNee's room, that her ideal thirteen-year-
old had been smoking cigarettes, she was, in her words,
crushed. "FaNee was such a perfect child before that,"
JoAnn Cooper said some time later. "She was angry
that we found out. She knew we knew that she had

done something we didn't approve of, and then the rebellion started. I was hurt. I was very hurt. I guess it
came through as disappointment."

Several months later, FaNee's grandmother died.
FaNee had been devoted to her grandmother. She wrote
a poem in her memory — an almost joyous poem,
filled with Christian faith in the afterlife ("Please
don't grieve over my happiness/Rejoice with me in the
presence of the Angels of Heaven"). She also took some
keepsakes from her grandmother's house, and was
apparently mortified when her parents found them and
explained that they would have to be returned. By then,
the Coopers were aware that FaNee was going to have a
difficult time as a teenager. They thought she might
be self-conscious about the double affliction of glasses
and braces. They thought she might be uncomfortable
in the role of the principal's daughter at Gresham. In
ninth grade, she entered Halls High School, where
JoAnn Cooper was teaching art. FaNee was a loner at
first. Then she fell in with what could only be considered a bad crowd.

Halls, a few miles to the north of Fountain City,
used to be known as Halls Crossroads. It is what Knoxville people call "over the ridge" — on the side of Black
Oak Ridge that has always been thought of as rural.
When FaNee entered Halls High, the Coopers were
already in the process of building a house on several
acres of land they had bought in Halls, in a sparsely
settled area along Brown Gap Road. Like two or three
other houses along the road, it was to be constructed
basically of huge logs taken from old buildings — a

house that Leo Cooper describes as being, like the name FaNee, "just a little bit different." Ten years ago, Halls Crossroads was literally a crossroads. Then some of the Knoxville expansion that had swollen Fountain City spilled over the ridge, planting subdivisions here and there on roads that still went for long stretches with nothing but an occasional house with a cow or two next to it. The increase in population did not create a town. Halls has no center. Its commercial area is a series of two or three shopping centers strung together on the Maynardville Highway, the four-lane that leads north into Union County — a place almost synonymous in east Tennessee with mountain poverty. Its restaurant is the Halls Freezo Drive-In. The gathering place for the group FaNee Cooper eventually found herself in was the Maynardville Highway Exxon station.

At Halls High School, the social poles were repre-sented by the Jocks and the Freaks. FaNee found her friends among the Freaks. "I am truly enlighted upon irregular trains of thought aimed at strange depots of mental wards," she wrote when she was fifteen. "Yes! Crazed farms for the mental off — Oh! I walked through the halls screams & loud laughter fill my ears — Orderlys try to reason with me — but I am unrea-sonable! The joys of being a FREAK in a circus of imagination." The little crowd of eight or ten young people that FaNee joined has been referred to by her mother as "the Union County group." A couple of the girls were from backgrounds similar to FaNee's, but all the boys had the characteristics, if not the precise addresses, that Knoxville people associate with the poor whites of Union County. They were the sort of boys who didn't bother to finish high school, or finished it in a special program for slow learners, or got ejected from it for taking a swing at the principal.

"I guess you can say they more or less dragged us down to their level with the drugs," a girl who was in the group — a girl who can be called Marcia — said recently. "And somehow we settled for it. It seems like we had to get ourselves in the pit before we could look out." People in the group used marijuana and Valium and LSD. They sneered at the Jocks and the "prim and proper little ladies" who went with the Jocks. "We set ourselves aside," Marcia now says. "We put ourselves above everyone. How we did that I don't know." In a Knox County high school, teenagers who want to get themselves in the pit need not mainline heroin. The Jocks they mean to be compared to do not merely show up regularly for classes and practice football and wear clean clothes; they watch their language and preach temperance and go to prayer meetings on Wednesday nights and talk about having a real good Christian witness. Around Knoxville, people who speak of well-behaved high-school kids often seem to use words like "perfect," or even "angels." For FaNee's group, the opposite was not difficult to figure out. "We were into wicked things, strange things," Marcia says. "It was like we were on some kind of devil trip." FaNee wrote about demons and vultures and rats. "Slithering serpents eat my sanity and bite my ass," she wrote in an essay called "The Lovely Road of Life," just after she turned sixteen, "while tornadoes derail and ever so swiftly destroy every car in my train of thought." She wrote a lot about death.

FaNee's girl friends spoke of her as "super-intelligent." Her English teacher found some of her writing profound — and disturbing. She was thought to be not just super-intelligent but super-mysterious, and even, at times, super-weird — an introverted girl who stared straight ahead with deep-brown, nearly black eyes and seemed to have thoughts she couldn't share. Nobody really knew why she had chosen to run with the Freaks — whether it was loneliness or rebellion or simple boredom. Marcia thought it might have had something to do with a feeling that her parents had settled on Kristy as their perfect child. "I guess she figured she couldn't be the best," Marcia said recently. "So she decided she might as well be the worst."

Toward the spring of FaNee's junior year at Halls, her problems seemed to deepen. Despite her intelligence, her grades were sliding. She was what her mother called "a mental dropout." Leo Cooper had to visit Halls twice because of minor suspensions. Once, FaNee had been caught smoking. Once, having ducked out of a required assembly, she was spotted by a favorite teacher, who turned her in. At home, she exchanged little more than short, strained formalities with Kristy, who shared their parents' opinion of FaNee's choice of friends. The Coopers had finished their house — a large house, its size accentuated by the huge old logs and a great stone fireplace and outsize "Paul Bunyan"-style furniture — but FaNee spent most of her time there in her own room, sleeping or listening to rock music through earphones. One night, there was a terrible scene when FaNee returned from a concert in a condition that Leo Cooper knew had to be the result of marijuana. JoAnn Cooper, who ordinarily strikes people as too gentle to raise her voice, found herself losing her temper regularly. Finally, Leo Cooper asked a counsellor he knew, Jim Griffin, to stop in at Halls High School and have a talk with FaNee — unofficially.

Griffin — a young man with a warm, informal manner — worked for the Juvenile Court of Knox County. He had a reputation for being able to reach teenagers who wouldn't talk to their parents or to school administrators. One Friday in March of 1977, he spent an hour and a half talking to FaNee Cooper. As Griffin recalls the interview, FaNee didn't seem alarmed by his presence. She seemed to him calm and controlled — Griffin thought it was something like talking to another adult — and, unlike most of the teenagers he dealt with, she looked him in the eye the entire time. Griffin, like some of FaNee's friends, found her eyes unsettling — "the coldest, most distant, but, at the same time, the most knowing eyes I'd ever seen." She expressed affection for her parents, but she didn't seem interested in exploring ways of getting along better with them. The impression she gave Griffin was that they were who they were, and she was who she was, and there didn't happen to be any connection. Several times, she made the same response to Griffin's suggestions: "It's too late."

*

That weekend, neither FaNee nor her parents brought up the subject of Griffin's visit. Leo Cooper has spoken of the weekend as being particularly happy; a friend of FaNee's who stayed over remembers it as particularly strained. FaNee stayed home from school on Monday because of a bad headache — she often had bad headaches — but felt well enough on Monday evening to drive to the library. She was to be home at nine. When she wasn't, Mrs. Cooper began to phone her friends. Finally, around ten, Leo Cooper got into his other car and took a swing around Halls — past the teenage hangouts like the Exxon station and the Pizza Hut and the Smoky Mountain Market. Then he took a second swing. At eleven, FaNee was still not home.

She hadn't gone to the library. She had picked up two girl friends and driven to the home of a third, where everyone took five Valium tablets. Then the four girls drove over to the Exxon station, where they met four boys from their crowd. After a while, the group bought some beer and some marijuana and reassembled at Charlie Stevens's trailer. Charlie Stevens was five or six years older than everyone else in the group — a skinny, slow-thinking young man with long black hair and a sparse beard. He was married and had a child, but he and his wife had separated; she was back in Union County with the baby. Stevens had remained in their trailer — parked in the yard near his mother's house, in a back-road area of Knox County dominated by decrepit, unpainted sheds and run-down trailers and rusted-out automobiles. Stevens had picked up FaNee at home once or twice — apparently, more as a driver for the group than as a date — and the Coopers, having learned that his unsuitability extended to being married, had asked her not to see him.

In Charlie's trailer, which had no heat or electricity, the group drank beer and passed around joints, keeping warm with blankets. By eleven or so, FaNee was what one of her friends has called "super-messed-up." Her speech was slurred. She was having trouble keeping her balance. She had decided not to go home. She had apparently persuaded herself that her parents intended to send her away to some sort of home for incorrigibles. "It's too late," she said to one of her friends. "It's just too late." It was decided that one of the boys, David Munsey, who was more or less the leader of the group, would drive the Coopers' car to FaNee's house, where FaNee and Charlie Stevens would pick him up in Stevens's car — a worn Pinto with four bald tires, one light, and a dragging muffler. FaNee wrote a note to her parents, and then, perhaps because her handwriting was suffering the effects of beer and marijuana and Valium, asked Stevens to rewrite it on a large piece of paper, which would be left on the seat of the Coopers' car. The Stevens version was just about the same as FaNee's, except that Stevens left out a couple of sentences about trying to work things out ("I'm willing to try") and, not having won any spelling championships himself, he misspelled a few words, like "tomorrow." The note said, "Dear Mom and Dad. Sorry I'm late. Very late. I left your car because I thought you might need it tomorrow. I love you all, but this is something I just had to do. The man talked to me privately for one and a half hours and I was really scared, so this is something I just had to do, but don't worry, I'm with a very good friend. Love you all. FaNee. P. S. Please try to understand I love you all very much, really I do. Love me if you have a chance."

At eleven-thirty or so, Leo Cooper was sitting in his living room, looking out the window at his driveway — a long gravel road that runs almost four hundred feet from the house to Brown Gap Road. He saw the car that FaNee had been driving pull into the driveway. "She's home," he called to his wife, who had just left the room. Cooper walked out on the deck over the garage. The car had stopped at the end of the driveway, and the lights had gone out. He got into his other car and drove to the end of the driveway. David Munsey had already joined Charlie Stevens and FaNee, and the Pinto was just leaving, travelling at a normal rate of speed. Leo Cooper pulled out on the road behind them.

Stevens turned left on Crippen Road, a road that has a field on one side and two or three small houses on the other, and there Cooper pulled his car in front of the Pinto and stopped, blocking the way. He got out and walked toward the Pinto. Suddenly, Stevens put the car in reverse, backed into a driveway a hundred yards behind him, and sped off. Cooper jumped in his car and gave chase. Stevens raced back to Brown Gap Road, ran a stop sign there, ran another stop sign at Maynardville Highway, turned north, veered off onto the old Andersonville Pike, a nearly abandoned road that runs parallel to the highway, and then crossed back over the highway to the narrow, dark country roads on the other side. Stevens sometimes drove with his lights out. He took some of the corners by suddenly applying his hand brake to make the car swerve around in a ninety-degree turn. He was in familiar territory — he actually passed his trailer — and Cooper had difficulty keeping up. Past the trailer, Stevens swept down a hill into a sharp left turn that took him onto Foust Hollow Road, a winding, hilly road not much wider than one car.

At a fork, Cooper thought he had lost the Pinto. He started to go right, and then saw what seemed to be a spark from Stevens's dragging muffler off to the left, in the darkness. Cooper took the left fork, down Salem Church Road. He went down a hill, and then up a long, curving hill to a crest, where he saw the Stevens car ahead. "I saw the car airborne. Up in the air," he later testified. "It was up in the air. And then it completely rolled over one more time. It started to make another flip forward, and just as it started to flip to the other side it flipped back this way, and my daughter's body came out."

Cooper slammed on his brakes and skidded to a stop up against the Pinto. "Book!" Stevens shouted — the group's equivalent of "Scram!" Stevens and Munsey disappeared into the darkness. "It was dark, no one around, and so I started yelling for FaNee," Cooper has testified. "I thought it was an eternity before I could find her body, wedged under the back end of

that car. . . . I tried everything I could, and saw that
I couldn't get her loose. So I ran to a trailer back up
to the top of the hill back up there to try to get that
lady to call to get me some help, and then apparently
she didn't think that I was serious. . . . I took the jack
out of my car and got under, and it was dark, still
couldn't see too much what was going on . . . and
started prying and got her loose, and I don't know how.
And then I dragged her over to the side, and, of course,
at the time I felt reasonably assured that she was gone,
because her head was completely — on one side just
as if you had taken a sledgehammer and just hit it
and bashed it in. And I did have the pleasure of one
thing. I had the pleasure of listening to her breathe
about the last three times she ever breathed in her
life."

David Munsey did not return to the wreck that night,
but Charlie Stevens did. Leo Cooper was kneeling next
to his daughter's body. Cooper insisted that Stevens
come close enough to see FaNee. "He was kneeling
down next to her," Stevens later testified. "And he said,
'Do you know what you've done? Do you really know
what you've done?' Like that. And I just looked at her,
and I said, 'Yes,' and just stood there. Because I
couldn't say nothing." There was, of course, a legal
decision to be made about who was responsible for
FaNee Cooper's death. In a deposition, Stevens said
he had been fleeing for his life. He testified that when
Leo Cooper blocked Crippen Road, FaNee had said

that her father had a gun and intended to hurt them. Stevens was bound over and eventually indicted for involuntary manslaughter. Leo Cooper testified that when he approached the Pinto on Crippen Road, FaNee had a strange expression that he had never seen before. "It wasn't like FaNee, and I knew something was wrong," he said. "My concern was to get FaNee out of the car." The district attorney's office asked that Cooper be bound over for reckless driving, but the judge declined to do so. "Any father would have done what he did," the judge said. "I can see no criminal act on the part of Mr. Cooper."

Almost two years passed before Charlie Stevens was brought to trial. Part of the problem was assuring the presence of David Munsey, who had joined the Navy but seemed inclined to assign his own leaves. In the meantime, the Coopers went to court with a civil suit — they had "uninsured-motorist coverage," which requires their insurance company to cover any defendant who has no insurance of his own — and they won a judgment. There were ways of assigning responsibility, of course, which had nothing to do with the law, civil or criminal. A lot of people in Knoxville thought that Leo Cooper had, in the words of his lawyer, "done what any daddy worth his salt would have done." There were others who believed that FaNee Cooper had lost her life because Leo Cooper had lost his temper. Leo Cooper was not among those who expressed any doubts about his actions. Unlike his wife, whose eyes filled with tears at almost any mention of FaNee,

Cooper seemed able, even eager to go over the details of the accident again and again. With the help of a school-board security man, he conducted his own investigation. He drove over the route dozens of times. "I've thought about it every day, and I guess I will the rest of my life," he said as he and his lawyer and the prosecuting attorney went over the route again the day before Charlie Stevens's trial finally began. "But I can't tell any alternative for a father. I simply wanted her out of that car. I'd have done the same thing again, even at the risk of losing her."

Tennessee law permits the family of a victim to hire a special prosecutor to assist the district attorney. The lawyer who acted for the Coopers in the civil case helped prosecute Charlie Stevens. Both he and the district attorney assured the jurors that the presence of a special prosecutor was not to be construed to mean that the Coopers were vindictive. Outside the courtroom, Leo Cooper said that the verdict was of no importance to him — that he felt sorry, in a way, for Charlie Stevens. But there were people in Knoxville who thought Cooper had a lot riding on the prosecution of Charlie Stevens. If Stevens was not guilty of FaNee Cooper's death — found so by twelve of his peers — who was?

At the trial, Cooper testified emotionally and remarkably graphically about pulling FaNee out from under the car and watching her die in his arms. Charlie Stevens had shaved his beard and cut his hair, but the effort did not transform him into an impressive witness. His lawyer — trying to argue that it would have been impossible for Stevens to concoct the story about FaNee's having mentioned a gun, as the prosecution strongly implied — said, "His mind is such that if you ask him a question you can hear his mind go around, like an old mill creaking." Stevens did not deny the recklessness of his driving or the sorry condition of his car. It happened to be the only car he had available to flee in, he said, and he had fled in fear for his life.

The prosecution said that Stevens could have let FaNee out of the car when her father stopped them, or could have gone to the commercial strip on the Maynardville Highway for protection. The prosecution said that Leo Cooper had done what he might have been expected to do under the circumstances — alone, late at night, his daughter in danger. The defense said precisely the same about Stevens: he had done what he might have been expected to do when being pursued by a man he had reason to be afraid of. "I don't fault Mr. Cooper for what he did, but I'm sorry he did it," the defense attorney said. "I'm sorry the girl said what she said." The jury deliberated for eighteen minutes. Charlie Stevens was found guilty. The jury recommended a sentence of from two to five years in the state penitentiary. At the announcement, Leo Cooper broke down and cried. JoAnn Cooper's eyes filled with tears; she blinked them back and continued to stare straight ahead.

*

In a way, the Coopers might still strike a casual visitor as an ideal family — handsome parents, a bright and bubbly teenage daughter, a little boy learning the hook shot from his father, a warm house with some land around it. FaNee's presence is there, of course. A picture of her, with a small bouquet of flowers over it, hangs in the living room. One of her poems is displayed in a frame on a table. Even if Leo Cooper continues to think about that night for the rest of his life, there are questions he can never answer. Was there a way that Leo and JoAnn Cooper could have prevented FaNee from choosing the path she chose? Would she still be alive if Leo Cooper had not jumped into his car and driven to the end of the driveway to investigate? Did she in fact tell Charlie Stevens that her father would hurt them — or even that her father had a gun? Did she want to get away from her family even at the risk of tearing around dark country roads in Charlie Stevens's dismal Pinto? Or did she welcome the risk? The poem of FaNee's that the Coopers have displayed is one she wrote a week before her death:

> I think I'm going to die
> And I really don't know why.
> But look in my eye
> When I tell you good-bye.
> I think I'm going to die.

Called at Rushton

Central Pennsylvania
November 1979

MARILYN MCCUSKER, a woman who had sued to
get her job in the Rushton coal mine, was killed one
afternoon this fall at the end of the eight-to-four shift.
She was working as a roof-bolter helper at the time —
placing long bolts in holes that a miner operating a
squat little forty-thousand-dollar machine drills straight
up every four feet to tighten the roof. The roof had
been re-bolted in an intersection next to a mined-out
area when Mrs. McCusker noticed some movement —
what miners mean when they say "the roof's working."
The roof-bolter made it out, but Mrs. McCusker was
pinned under an eighteen-foot section of roof. She was
not crushed. No bones were broken. The death cer-
tificate said that she died of shock and asphyxiation.
Although the reports being prepared by various agencies on the accident have not been completed, it is
believed that one of Mrs. McCusker's knees was bent
upward against her windpipe. She had been a miner
for almost exactly two years. In 1975, she and three
other women had sued the Rushton Mining Company,

claiming that they had been denied employment on
the basis of their sex. The suit was filed only a few
months after Marilyn McCusker, then Marilyn Williams, moved to the central-Pennsylvania mining country from Utica, New York. The possibility of applying
for work at Rushton had been brought up by a friend
named Mary Louise Carson, who was prompted to
apply because her sister-in-law was already working
as a coal miner in another mine and her husband was
not working at all. "If you don't have money, you die
in this country," Mary Louise Carson said later. "You
can't survive."

People who knew Marilyn Williams at the time say
that she probably went with Mary Louise Carson to file
a coal-miner application because she was game. "She
was the sort of person who'd say 'Sure — O.K.' if someone got the idea at the last minute to go to the movies,"
one of them said recently. As it happens, the movie
house in Coalport, where she lived, has been closed
for years. Moving to Coalport could qualify as game in
itself. It is a small, gray town in a part of central
Pennsylvania where the towns tend to be small and
gray and to have movie houses that have been closed
for years. Just outside Coalport, the view of the surrounding mountains can be spectacular, unless it happens to include one whose top was lopped off by a
strip miner who managed to go bankrupt before the
time came to reclaim the mined-out land. From the
main street of Coalport — a line of dark taverns and
fitfully open stores — the mountain that dominates

the view is a mountain of spoil left from an abandoned mine called the Sunshine. Apparently, Marilyn Williams moved to Coalport because it happened to be the home town of a fellow worker at a Masonic nursing home in Utica, New York, where both of them were employed as nurse's aides, and she happened to be at a point in her life when she wanted to live anywhere but Utica, New York. She was thirty, divorced, rather high-strung. She spoke very quickly, and she was quick to smile. She looked, according to one friend, "like someone's third-grade teacher." She brought her son, Michael, then twelve, along with her. A visitor standing on the main street of town can easily assume that the story of postwar Coalport in-migration begins and ends with their arrival.

Mary Louise Carson had heard, apparently incorrectly, that the federal government had told Rushton to begin hiring some women. To a lot of working people in towns like Coalport, male as well as female, it must sometimes seem as if something on the order of federal intervention is necessary to get a job in a deep mine. It is common for people to put in an application at several mines — mines that might be forty or fifty miles from where they live — and then wait to be "called." A conversation in one of the dark taverns of Coalport or Osceola Mills or Houtzdale sometimes sounds like the conversation at a conference of Baptist preachers — the man at the end of the bar talking about the time he was called at Bethlehem, the bartender speaking of someone who was called at

Barnes & Tucker. The deep mines in central Pennsylvania are unionized, and the union scale for a coal miner is about nine and a half dollars an hour. The only other hourly wages in the area that approach nine and a half dollars are paid in strip mines — where job security is limited not only by the lack of a union but by the tendency of strip-mine entrepreneurs to take leave of the business without much warning. For some years, the coal industry has not been thriving, a condition that just about everyone in central Pennsylvania — labor and management and chamber of commerce and bystander — tends to blame on outlandish restrictions by the Environmental Protection Agency. These days, it is not uncommon for someone to have had applications on file with four or five mines for years. Alan McCusker, the young man Marilyn Williams married a year or so after she arrived in Coalport, says that he had an application in at Rushton himself at the time his future wife applied. Rushton is the deep mine most convenient to Coalport. It also has the stability that comes with being what is known as a captive mine — a mine whose entire production is used by its owner, in this case a utility in the northeastern part of the state called Pennsylvania Power & Light. Alan McCusker was never called at Rushton. The response to the application of Marilyn Williams and the women who went with her was more clear-cut: the superintendent of the Rushton mine, Blair Rickard, told them that there would be women miners in his mine over his dead body.

Eventually, the mining company settled the suit out of court, agreeing to hire all four women and to award them back pay. While the case was in court, there were rumors that the plaintiffs had been recruited by a lawyer from some women's-liberation outfit, but the rumors were untrue. They had found their own lawyer, Mary Ellen Krober, a young woman from Carlisle who was recommended by a local legal-aid attorney. Their interests were not ideological but financial. Nearly all the women who started working at the Rushton mine in 1977 were the breadwinners of their families. Alan McCusker has worked at a number of jobs, but never at one for a number of years. Bernice Dombroski, who had applied at Rushton without knowing about the suit and was called before the litigants were, is married to a man who is partly disabled and who works only seasonally. "If we had to live on what he makes," she said not long ago, "we'd starve to death."

Before the settlement, Marilyn McCusker worked for a while in a local nursing home. Mary Louise Carson worked in a clothing factory. Neither of them made more than the minimum wage. "A lot of people in the sewing factory said I was crazy to apply to the mine," Mrs. Carson told a visitor recently. "But the sewing factory was a sweatshop. I heard of people there having nervous breakdowns. You don't know what a woman has to do." Spending all day at a sewing machine can make a coal miner's job seem almost liberating — particularly when it pays nine and a half dollars an hour. "I like it down there," Mrs. Carson, the only original litigant left among the three women who now work at Rushton, said recently. "It's a different world." It's a dirty world, of course — so dirty that coal miners have to use Ivory Liquid rather than bath soap when they finish a shift. It is often uncomfortable. It is always dangerous. Within the first few months at Rushton, Marilyn McCusker's nose was broken by a pipe and her arm was wrenched when her shovel got caught in the belt that carries the coal out of the mine. Alan McCusker says that his wife was going to quit coal mining as soon as he completed a house he was building for the family across the road from where they lived, but he also says that her proudest day was the day when, after a year at Rushton, she won her mining papers and was able to trade the yellow hat of a "greenie" for the black hat of a certified miner. "She loved it from the first day," he said recently. "It's dirty and dark and rats running around all over the place. All her life, though, basically she'd never had a good day's pay. She was just doing menial work. When she came back the first day, she was smiling from ear to ear. She just loved it."

Even when the suit was settled, Blair Rickard never pretended to welcome women in his coal mine. Although Rushton picked up a small reputation for innovation a couple of years ago by experimenting with an "autonomous mining" program that gave work crews some say in how the day's work should be approached — the program was eventually voted out by the union — Blair Rickard is an old-fashioned mine superintendent. Except for one six-month period spent wiring buildings, he has been in coal mining since he got out of high school, in 1937. He has worked as a miner "at the face" with a pick and shovel. He has worked as a foreman. He has run his own small mine. He is known as a strong churchgoer who believes that women would have no place in a coal mine even if they could do a man's work. "Honest to God, I love the woman," he said recently. "I respect the woman as a lady. I kind of look up to 'em. I know they have to find their way in society, but there's just oodles of jobs for women — like office jobs. I'm a hundred per cent against 'em in a coal mine. They just can't do the work. We're paying them women to get them off our back is all we're doing."

These days, coal is gouged out of the face of a mine with a ferocious device called a continuous-mining machine, rather than with a pick and shovel. The women who work underground claim that the physical labor is no more strenuous than moving aside a couch for a vacuum cleaner or lugging around a husky three-year-old. "It just ain't hard work," according to Mary Ann Baum, a woman who worked at Rushton until recently. Male miners, though, tend to believe that women cannot do the job — cannot handle the sections of tree trunk that are used as props for the roof of the mine, cannot run complicated equipment like the continuous miner, cannot carry their share of rail or heavy pipe. (Blair Rickard acknowledges that there are a few jobs that women could do as well as men if only they were willing to work — including bolter helper, the job Marilyn McCusker was doing when she was killed — but he believes them incapable of running machines, and he doesn't think many of them really are willing to work.) A lot of people in central Pennsylvania, male and female, agree with Rickard that a coal mine is simply no place for a woman. "I wouldn't let my wife down there," a former miner who has sons in the mines said recently. "I'd break her leg first." Some people believe that, apart from the matter of efficiency and propriety, having women in a coal mine is bad luck — or worse luck, really, since working eight hours a day in a place where people are regularly killed or crippled might be considered bad luck to begin with. Miners have generally accepted the fact that equal-employment laws mean the inevitability of women in the mines — many male miners, in fact, have been helpful to the women who do get hired — but nobody pretends that male miners are much more enthusiastic about the presence of women than Rickard is. "Some of the men are O.K.," Mrs. Carson has said. "But some of 'em goes up your one side and down the other. They don't want us in there."

"As far as Rushton's concerned, the women's always going to have problems," Bernice Dombroski says. She blames the problems not on the men but on Blair Rickard. Women who work at Rushton claim that in matters like shift assignments or certification for mining papers Rickard favors his friends and relatives over anyone else, and anyone else over a woman. They claim that the United Mine Workers of America local at Rushton is not very useful in protecting their rights

— and is too cozy with management in general. ("Rushton's more like a scab hole.") However angry women like Bernice Dombroski and Mary Louise Carson may sound at times, though, they do not think of themselves as militants — and certainly not as feminists. "I believe if a woman does the work she ought to get the pay," Mrs. Carson says. "But I don't believe in women football players or homosexuals or abortion." Although Bernice Dombroski has a sweatshirt that says "When God Created Man, She Was Only Joking," the sweatshirt is itself meant as a joke. "I don't go along with women's lib or homosexuals or nothing like that," she says. "They're for a lot of things I'm against."

Although Rickard cannot find anything to compliment about Marilyn McCusker's productivity as a coal miner beyond a pleasing personality and a good attendance record, he admits that Bernice Dombroski is one female miner who does her job as well as a man. "I can throw them props as good as any man down there," she said recently. "One of the guys taught me how to sling them over your shoulder." She is a blunt, rough-talking woman who grew up in Coalport, one of sixteen children of a miner at the old Sunshine mine. She is accustomed to taking care of herself. She was Marilyn McCusker's best friend at the mine ("We had a lot in common; we both had hard lives"), and she urged upon her friend the Bernice Dombroski method for getting along with abusive fellow workers — "You give it back, they'll leave you alone." She gets along with her fellow workers pretty well herself — partly, she says, "because I talk like them and I can cuss them out." Her response to hearing that some miners' wives are concerned about their husbands' working in such close quarters with women is likely to be rude remarks about how few of the men she works with would provide significant temptation. Before Mrs. Dombroski started working at Rushton, Blair Rickard lectured his miners about the necessity of modifying their language a bit. "Wouldn't you know it?" he said recently. "It wasn't two weeks before I had her in this office telling her she was embarrassing my men the way she talked." It may have been the first time in the history of the American coal industry that anyone was officially chastised for using strong language in a coal mine.

Alan McCusker stopped work on the new house for a time, but he has now started again. He and his late wife's son, Michael Williams, still live in a small frame house across the road — a house built by McCusker's grandfather, who worked at the Sunshine mine. A couple of weeks after the accident, the mining-company official in charge of workmen's compensation phoned to say that he wanted to drop by to explain some differences in the death-benefits claim that arose from McCusker's being a widower rather than a widow. McCusker thought the official meant differences in wording — changing a "his" to a "her" now and then — but it turned out that the difference referred to was a section of the Pennsylvania workmen's-compensation law that says a widower is entitled to full benefits only if he is incapable of supporting himself and was dependent upon the worker who was killed. McCusker, who is twenty-eight and able-bodied, responded by accusing the company of attempting to treat his wife unequally in death as well as in life. "Marilyn didn't win everything she thought she did," he said. "The legal battle may not be over."

It has been a month since Marilyn McCusker was killed, and the Rushton mine has, of course, long been back in normal operation. The normal operation, though, remains something of a disappointment to Blair Rickard. For some time, the mine has not been meeting his expectations. A bonus plan was put in last spring — a plan that means additional pay for just about everyone in any month when the production of clean coal exceeds about twenty-five hundred tons a day — but the production has met the bonus requirement only once. There have been a lot of equipment breakdowns. There have been the usual problems with absenteeism, particularly on Friday swing shifts. Another miner was killed in July, crushed under a machine he was trying to repair. At times, Rickard connects the problems of the mine with the hiring of women. "It seems to be a jinx," he said recently. "The mine ain't been the same since they came." After Marilyn McCusker's death, Mary Louise Carson says, the mine's front-office secretary asked all the remaining women miners whether or not they intended to quit. "I told her I wasn't planning on it," Mrs. Carson said not long ago. "The men don't quit if one of their buddies gets hurt. If they had the choice — if they could make the money outside — there'd be nobody in that mine."

Resettling the Yangs

Fairfield, Iowa
March 1980

As a REFUGE, Fairfield, Iowa, has a lot going for it. To Theng Pao Yang and his wife and their four children, who arrived in Fairfield at the beginning of December from Laos by way of a refugee camp in Thailand, it might have looked like any other frigid and startlingly foreign place, but, as the fortunes of Southeast Asian refugees go, the Yang family could have been considered fortunate. The entire state of Iowa seems to have taken upon itself a special responsibility for Southeast Asian refugees. The one state agency among the American organizations resettling refugees from the camps is the Iowa Refugee Service Center. When the nations of the world were trying to decide what to do about the boat people, the governor of Iowa announced that Iowa would take fifteen hundred of them. Iowa's response to reports of widespread starvation among Cambodian refugees in Thailand was to raise more than five hundred thousand dollars in small donations and dispatch what amounted to an Iowa relief column with food and supplies, accompanied by a *Des Moines Register* and *Tribune* reporter to make certain that it reached the people it was intended for. There are, of course, Iowans who believe that the United States should concentrate on the problems of its own citizens instead of worrying so much about displaced Asians — a *Register* poll last year indicated that a shade over half the people in the state were opposed to resettling more boat people in Iowa — but they have not been outspoken about their reservations. The dominant attitude in Iowa toward refugees seems to combine spontaneous generosity and genuine concern and great pride in the leadership Iowa has taken. Asked to account for all of this, Michael Gartner, the editor of the *Register* and of the *Tribune,* tends to smile and say, "Iowa has a better foreign policy than the United States."

Fairfield is a pleasant town of eight thousand people in the southeast corner of the state. It remains financially comfortable through trade with the area's hog-and-grain farmers and the presence of a dozen manufacturing plants and the official business of Jefferson County — conducted out of a magnificent pile of a courthouse that was built in 1891. Fairfield people are accustomed to strangers. In the sixties, the local college, Parsons, was transformed into an education mill that became known nationally as Flunk-Out U. The campus now belongs to Maharishi International University, where students of Transcendental Meditation are said to be instructed in arts that include human levitation — although, as one of the hog-and-grain farmers might say, not so's you'd know it. When the Yangs arrived in Fairfield, there were already three Laotian refugee families in town — ethnic-Lao families from the lowlands — and another arrived a couple of weeks later. The men in the Laotian families were already employed. The older children were in school. Daily English classes had been established for some time in a room at the First Lutheran church. While the adults learned English, Fairfield volunteers acted as babysitters for their small children.

In Fairfield, it is natural for Christian charity to be channelled through a church. Sponsoring a Southeast Asian refugee family began as a commitment taken on at one church or another, but it quickly turned ecumenical. The sponsorship of the first Laotians to arrive in town — Kesone Sisomphane and his family, who came only last spring — passed from the Episcopal priest to the Lutheran pastor when the Episcopalian moved away. A widower and his children from Vientiane were sponsored by the First United Methodist Church through the Catholic resettlement agency and eventually decided to attend Sunday services with the Lutherans. Sponsors shared ideas and problems, and the refugees seemed as compatible as the sponsors. When congregants of the First Lutheran Church decided to sponsor a refugee family — the family, as it turned out, that arrived just after the Yangs — the Lutheran pastor, Keith Lingwall, specifically asked for lowland Lao in order to preserve the homogeneity of the group.

The Fairfield church that sponsored the Yang family, First Baptist, is considerably smaller than the congregations that were already working together with the Laotians. As an American Baptist rather than a Southern Baptist congregation, it is not opposed to ecumenism. Its pastor, Lynn Bergfalk — who, like Keith Lingwall, is in his thirties and bearded and well educated — has served as president of the Fairfield ministerial alliance. Still, there remain limitations on the Baptists' ecumenical participation, and there remains in the minds of other Fairfield Christians some residue of the old notion that Baptists tend to stand a bit apart. Among the refugees in Fairfield, Theng Pao Yang and his family stood more than a bit apart. Although they came from Laos, the Yangs were not lowland Lao-speakers but Hmong — members of a mountain tribe that has had trouble with the dominant Lao for as long as anybody can remember.

In Laos, the Hmong were always called Meo, which means "barbarians" — a name they understandably despise. The Hmong originated in southern China, and over the past century or so many of them have migrated into the highlands of northern Laos and Thailand. To readers of *National Geographic* articles, they were mountain tribesmen in intricate ceremonial costumes — deft with the crossbow, surefooted on mountain paths, skilled at coaxing a steady opium crop out of the steep hillsides, persistent in their animism despite some conversions to Buddhism and Christianity. To military men in Laos, the Hmong had a considerable reputation as guerrilla fighters; there were Hmong forces in the Pathet Lao and in the Royal Laotian Army and particularly in the secret army financed by the Central Intelligence Agency. In Laos, the Hmong have sometimes been considered naïve hillbillies — people subjected to ridicule or harassment or even extortion.

To refugee workers — such as those in the American Baptist Churches resettlement office, which received the Yangs as part of its refugee allotment from Church World Service — the Hmong are known for being close-knit, even clannish people who seek each other out through a tribal communication system that sometimes seems to work almost as well in California or Pennsylvania as it did in the mountains of Southeast Asia. The Yangs had requested resettlement in Iowa because of a friend they mentioned as living in the northeast part of the state — in a town that did not, as it happened, have a Baptist church to act as a sponsor for the family. In Fairfield, a hundred and fifty miles to the south, First Baptist, which had sponsored a Burmese technician and his wife who immigrated in 1975, was eager to sponsor a refugee family. Although the Baptist resettlement office was aware that some antipathy exists between Hmong and Lao, the antipathy had never been considered serious enough to require segregation. The presence of any Laotians in Fairfield — their ethnic background was unknown to the resettlement office — had been considered an attraction: it meant that the town was used to refugees and had some facilities in place for them.

No one in Fairfield knew much about the Hmong.

The Iowa Refugee Service Center, which does employment and social-service work among refugees as well as resettling, had pamphlets on Hmong culture and a Hmong outreach worker on its staff and knowledge of some Hmong families in Ottumwa, only twenty-five miles from Fairfield, but First Baptist was not in touch with the Iowa Refugee Service Center. There did not seem to be any need for out-of-town assistance. Theng Pao Yang spoke and understood some Lao, so communication was possible through the Laotians who were available every day at English class. A lot of communication was possible through sign language. The church installed the Yangs in a small bungalow that was empty while on the market to be sold. The two older children, an eight-year-old boy named So and a six-year-old girl named Bay, were enrolled at Roosevelt Elementary School and given individual tutoring in English. Theng Pao Yang's wife, Yi Ly, was taken to the doctor for a checkup. The Burmese who had immigrated five years ago began taking the family to the supermarket once a week. After a week or two, the main burden of transporting the family and looking after its daily needs passed from Lynn Bergfalk to a warm and cheerful couple from the congregation — John Heckenberg, a recently retired postal worker, and his wife, Madelon, both of whom had spent the first thirty or so years of their lives on an Iowa farm. John Heckenberg drove the Yangs to English class. Madelon Heckenberg did the Yangs' family laundry in her automatic washer. Even without a common language, Madelon Heckenberg and the Yangs had what she calls "regular laugh sessions."

What Madelon Heckenberg knew about Hmong in general she heard from Kesone Sisomphane, the best English-speaker among the Laotian refugees, who told her that they were rather primitive — a remark she took as "sort of a put-down." Other people active in Fairfield refugee work took similar remarks as a natural enough effort on the part of the Lao to distance themselves from people who might make a bad impression on the hosts — or even as a way of pointing out that adjustment might be more difficult for people who had never driven a car or operated a typewriter or spoken some French. To the English teacher, Barbara Hill, it appeared that the other Laotians were trying to help Theng Pao Yang and his family — trying to include them in the joking that sometimes went on in class, trying to commiserate with them when they were sad. Theng Pao was often sad. In English class, he sometimes began sobbing.

One of the Lao explained to Mrs. Hill that Theng Pao was sad about having to leave his parents behind in the refugee camp. It was apparent that the contrast between life in Fairfield and the life the Yangs had left behind was strong enough to be upsetting. The Yangs had been in a refugee camp for five years. The biographical document that had been sent from Thailand on the Yangs summed up the schooling of all members of the family in one word: None. Mrs. Hill, through Kesone Sisomphane, explained to Yi Ly, through Theng Pao, that nursing a child publicly might be considered provocative rather than natural by some American men — an explanation Kesone Sisomphane carried out with dramatic warnings about locking doors and pulling shades. When So and Bay were being registered in school, Theng Pao seemed bewildered, and eventually walked off to squat silently in the hall. Although So, who was more outgoing than Bay, seemed to be responding particularly well to Roosevelt, the two younger children seemed frightened of everybody except their mother — a fact that made for some disturbance in the English class. At first, Mrs. Hill's main concern was for Yi Ly — who appeared troubled, and burdened with her babies — but gradually it turned toward Theng Pao.

Although Yi Ly began joining in the classroom joking, Theng Pao often seemed to retreat within himself, chewing nervously on his pencil. He sometimes seemed upset by having the members of his family separated for any reason. He said, through the Lao, that he didn't understand why he couldn't have a telephone. (First Baptist had decided that it would be wasteful to pay for installing a telephone in a house that might be sold at any time — particularly considering the fact that the Yangs could not speak English and might even be alarmed by a wrong number.) An attempt to find Theng Pao a job at a local plant that employed two of the Laotians as sweepers proved unsuccessful. The personnel man found him distracted and asked Mrs. Hill if there was anything wrong with

him. Mrs. Hill did not believe that there was anything
wrong with Theng Pao — or anything serious enough
to bring to the attention of Lynn Bergfalk. Theng Pao
was, after all, in a difficult position — suddenly placed
in a strange country, where he could communicate
with his hosts only through a third language. He presumably did have relatives who had been left behind.
He was less equipped to deal with the shock of modern
America than the urban Lao were. Mrs. Hill simply
thought he would be slower to adapt. Lynn Bergfalk
had seen Theng Pao cry a couple of times, but why
shouldn't a man in his situation cry? With the Heckenbergs, the Yangs seemed all smiles and genuine affection. "They just smiled," Madelon Heckenberg has said.
"It was easy to work with them, because they appre-
ciated what you did for them. That family wanted to
please more than anybody I ever heard of."

On a cold Thursday in January, Su Thao, the Hmong
outreach worker at the Iowa Refugee Service Center,
happened to be calling on a Hmong family in northeast
Iowa. He was shown a letter from Theng Pao Yang,
who had written that he was homesick and wanted to
move in order to be with other Hmong. The next day,
Su Thao drove to Fairfield to look in on the Yangs.
Theng Pao cried when he saw Su Thao. He told Su
Thao that he wanted to move to California, where he
had a first cousin. Su Thao tried to comfort Theng Pao.
He said there were seven hundred and fifty Hmong in
Iowa, some of them as close as Ottumwa. He told him
that the people at First Baptist were obviously atten-

tive and caring sponsors. He told him that the Yangs would be wise to remain in Fairfield, where there were people committed to helping them, at least until Theng Pao learned some English. Su Thao did not consider Theng Pao's mood alarming. He had seen a lot of home-sick refugees. He had seen a lot of refugees who did not have sponsors as attentive as the people from First Baptist. The family he had been calling on when he heard about the Yangs had been brought to Iowa by a man and wife who then decided to get a divorce. Su Thao left Theng Pao his office telephone number and his home telephone number.

The Tuesday after Su Thao's visit turned out to be a day with a lot of changes in the Yangs' regular sched-ule. The eight-year-old boy, So, was taken to the dentist to have a tooth pulled. In English class, Mrs. Hill an-nounced that the students would begin coming at two different times so that she could divide up what amounted to the elementary and intermediate speak-ers. That evening, the Heckenbergs, who had learned of an out-of-town funeral they would have to attend, realized that the laundry they would have ordinarily delivered the next day might be needed before they returned from their trip; John Heckenberg drove over to the Yangs' with it. He found Yi Ly distraught. Her son, So, was lying on the living-room sofa. The boy's eyes were closed. He was cold to the touch. Theng Pao and Bay seemed to be moaning or grieving in the bed-room. Heckenberg, seeing no light on in nearby houses, drove home, and his wife phoned Lynn Bergfalk, who phoned for an ambulance. Theng Pao and Bay turned out to have been moaning not out of grief but because of serious injury. They were rushed to the Jefferson County Hospital and then taken by air ambulance to a hospital in Iowa City. So was pronounced dead at the scene.

It was not at all clear what had happened. Yi Ly, of course, spoke only Hmong. Finally, she pulled Madelon Heckenberg out of the crowd in the bungalow's tiny living room and led her down into the basement. Some of the Yangs' possessions were on the floor: five dollars in American bills that had been cut up with scissors, a Hmong flute that had been shattered, a knife whose blade had been broken. Over a pipe, there were six cords with nooses tied in them.

Yi Ly told two or three stories — in sign language then, in Hmong later to Su Thao, who had hurried down from Des Moines to interpret — but the one the Department of Criminal Investigation and the county attorney came to believe was that the entire Yang family, upon the decision of Theng Pao and with the acquiescence of Yi Ly, had tried to commit suicide — with the parents hanging the children who were too young to hang themselves. Apparently, Yi Ly had changed her mind at the last minute, and had finally managed to cut everyone down — too late for So. If John Heckenberg had not happened to walk in with the laundry, the authorities believed, it might have been too late for Theng Pao and Bay as well.

Theng Pao, rambling and incoherent in his hospital room, had even more stories than Yi Ly. He said that his dead sister had asked him to join her. He said Jesus had given him orders. He said one of the children had broken the case of First Baptist's tape player, and the Yangs were afraid their sponsors would no longer love them. He said that he had read in a book that they would all die anyway. Eventually, Theng Pao and Yi Ly offered a story that caused consternation among the churchgoing people of Fairfield: they said that Theng Pao had acted because of a threat from the lowland Lao. The threat they related was specific. Theng Pao would be killed. The Lao men would sleep with Yi Ly. The children would be divided up among the Lao families. Yi Ly would be married to the widower from Vientiane whom the Methodists had brought to Fairfield.

To Lynn Bergfalk, it was the first explanation that made sense. "The whole situation, from my perspective, is that the hanging is totally inexplicable unless there was an external factor like a death threat," he told the local paper. "They were a happy family, with no reason to do something like this." To the sponsors of the lowland-Lao families, it was an explanation that made no sense at all. The Lao all denied that anybody had said anything that could even have been misconstrued as a threat. Their sponsors believed them. They pointed out that the Lao had visited the Yangs two or three times, that Theng Pao had used the widower's phone to call his cousin in California, that the Lao families had been present, taking snapshots, when the Yangs were visited by friends from northeast Iowa. The Lao's sponsors were concerned that the Lao were being unfairly maligned and perhaps even endangered: a number of out-of-town Hmong, the noted guerrilla fighters, had begun to show up in Fairfield to see if they could be of assistance. Lynn Bergfalk said it was nonsense for anybody to be concerned about the possibility of retaliation, but for a week or so after the hangings Lao women who were alone while their husbands worked night shifts found themselves with visitors from among the sponsors. Some people in Fairfield thought that what the Baptists had found — during a time when they could be expected to be feeling both grief-stricken and guilty — was not an explanation but a scapegoat. Some Baptists thought that the other sponsors were refusing to consider the possibility that their refugees could lie to them — that Theng Pao and Yi Ly had been telling the truth. As positions hardened, Keith Lingwall, a pastor who is friendly by nature and ecumenical by policy, found himself uncomfortable in the presence of Lynn Bergfalk.

The county attorney of Jefferson County, a young man named Edwin F. Kelly, found himself with a complicated legal situation. He was satisfied, after a time, that he knew what had happened that night at the Yangs' bungalow, but he was not optimistic about finding out for certain exactly why it happened. He could find no evidence, other than the story told by the Yangs, that a threat had been involved. That still left the question of whether to prosecute Theng Pao and Yi Ly — both of whom had presumably tried to hang their children as well as themselves. Some of the people involved in Iowa refugee work contended that, considering the unchallenged authority of the father in a Hmong household, Yi Ly could hardly have been expected to do other than her husband had instructed her to do. Kelly believed that both Theng Pao and Yi Ly were lacking in what lawyers call *mens rea* — criminal intent. There was another consideration that weighed heavily with Kelly. Whatever crime had been committed had been committed against the children, and Kelly believed that the deportation of the Yang family — an inevitable consequence of a felony conviction — would bring the victims not justice but simply more suffering.

Among the material furnished him by the Iowa Refugee Service Center, Kelly came across a paper by a San Francisco psychologist named J. Donald Cohon which dealt with instances of "trauma syndrome" found in refugees throughout the world. Kelly underlined some of the symptoms of trauma syndrome that were familiar from the investigation of what Theng Pao had been like around the time of the hanging — paranoid tendencies, for instance, and inability to concentrate and loss of appetite and fear that something could happen to members of his family. Kelly's presentation to the grand jury stressed the possibility that

Theng Pao had been suffering from trauma syndrome, and that, Theng Pao being Yi Ly's only source of information in Fairfield, his version of reality had become her own. The grand jury returned no indictment. The Yangs were resettled among Hmong in another part of the state, in an arrangement that included some outside supervision of their children. It seemed a humane, Iowa sort of solution — what Keith Lingwall has called "a kind door-closing on a sad and tragic situation." There were presumably people in Fairfield who believed that the Yangs had got off too easy, but, like the people in Iowa with doubts about whether refugees should be there in the first place, they did not make a public issue of it. Everybody seemed satisfied. The way some of the Baptists would describe Kelly's solution, though, was not as a kind door-closing but as "a convenient answer that lets everybody off the hook."

"It's easier for everyone else to say 'Let's end this chapter,' " Bergfalk said recently. In the view of some Baptists, the people of Fairfield, comfortable with their humane solution, ended the chapter without investigating thoroughly enough the possibility that Theng Pao Yang was driven to his appalling decision by a threat. Although Lynn Bergfalk has not made any accusations against the Lao families personally, it is apparent to his colleagues in the ministry that he has never accepted Kelly's notion that what Theng Pao did can be explained by a paper written by a psychologist in San Francisco. The reluctance of the Baptists to discount the possibility that the Lao played some role in So Yang's death was bolstered by the Hmong who came to Fairfield just after the incident. To them, the threat Theng Pao described had a dreadful resonance. "It's the sort of thing that would happen at home," Tou-Fu Vang, a Hmong leader, said recently. To Tou-Fu Vang, the fact that the Lao visited the Yang family is not an indication that they were friendly but an indication that they had designs on Yi Ly. Why else would Lao visit Hmong?

Publicly, there is no argument in Fairfield about the Yangs. Privately, there are hard feelings. A Methodist refers to the Yangs' sponsors as "those Baptist people" in the same tone the Lao might use to speak of Hmong. A little girl who goes to the Methodist church is upset because a Baptist friend says, "That old man your church brought caused all the trouble." A clergyman like Keith Lingwall is troubled because he realizes that the door never quite closed. "I need to go visit with Lynn," Lingwall said not long ago. He did, but the visit did not change the views of either of them. "The truth, no matter how unpleasant, has to be faced," Lynn Bergfalk has said. There are expressions of compassion in Fairfield for the anguish the Baptists must have suffered over the death of So Yang, but there is also talk about what the Baptists might have done wrong — the possibility that they "smothered" the Yangs or treated them like pets, the possibility that Theng Pao's self-respect was threatened, the possibility that the Yangs were insulted rather than pleased at, say, having their laundry done for them. There are people in Fairfield who, out of irritation with the Baptists or a paucity of Christian charity or a sincere belief that they are facing an unpleasant truth, say that So Yang would be alive today if the Baptists had been willing to risk having to pay an extra installation charge on a telephone.

Nobody knows, of course, whether a telephone would have made any difference. Nobody knows what caused Theng Pao to decide that he and his family should die. In Fairfield, though, there is no shortage of theories. It may have been, some people say, that Theng Pao, in addition to his other problems, was suffering from an awful failure in communication. What he heard from his hosts, after all, went from English to someone who only began learning English last spring, then into Lao that Theng Pao may have understood imperfectly. Perhaps Kesone Sisomphane's dramatic message about breast-feeding gradually grew in Theng Pao's mind into the impression that his wife was going to be abducted. Perhaps, through the muddle of languages or his own disorientation, what Theng Pao understood from the changes announced in English class that day was that he had somehow been rejected as a student of English. Perhaps the notion that everyone would die anyway had come from a Lao New Testament Bergfalk had given him. It is possible to envision Theng Pao as someone trapped in a horrifying isolation — receiving information only through the short circuits of half-understood languages and his own confusion, communicating only through people he mistrusted. It is possible to envision him entertaining friends or talking to his first cousin in California on the telephone. It may be that Theng Pao Yang, bewildered and unsure of the language, understood a joke, perhaps even a cruel joke, as a threat. It may be that Theng Pao was in fact threatened with death by the Lao. It may be that he was suffering from trauma syndrome.

"We were doing everything we knew how," Madelon Heckenberg said recently. "Maybe we just didn't have the know-how." Lynn Bergfalk has given a lot of thought to what the First Baptist Church might have done differently in its sponsorship of the Yangs — whether finding a Hmong interpreter at the beginning would have made any difference, whether searching out the Hmong families in Ottumwa would have made any difference. He has given a lot of thought to whether or not a tendency to believe in the likelihood of some external factor like a threat is simply a way of dealing with feelings of guilt. National agencies involved with the resettlement of the Yangs are considering the possibility that Hmong ought to be settled only in clusters and that sponsors ought to be more carefully briefed on the cultural background of arriving refugees and that refugee agencies ought to figure out how to communicate with each other more effectively. The people in Fairfield who noticed some signs of stress in Theng

Pao wonder what might have happened if they had expressed serious concern to his sponsors, who saw only smiles. "We every last one of us feel guilty about this," Barbara Hill said recently. It may be, of course, that there is no reason for anyone to feel guilty. No isolated Hmong has ever before attempted suicide. What would the Baptists have done differently if they had been experts in Hmong culture? Perhaps what happened to the Yangs was caused by something from their past in Asia. Perhaps it came from a combination of the reasons people in Fairfield have offered — or from none of them at all. Barbara Hill sometimes thinks that the Asians she teaches are not as intent as Westerners on finding reasons for everything. "We can't tolerate a void," she said not long ago. "We have to find a cause. It may be that we're trying to find reasons for something Theng Pao never intended there to be a reason for."

Among Friends

Savannah, Georgia
February 1981

PUBLICLY, George Mercer IV was reported missing
on February 7, 1980. His picture ran above a small
item in both the *Savannah Morning News* and *Evening
Press*. The item said he had been missing since January 29th. It described him as being twenty-two years
old, five feet eight inches tall, about a hundred and
fifty-five pounds. It asked anyone having information
about him to telephone the Savannah Police Department. The picture showed a young man with the sort
of thick mustache and blow-dried hair that make a
lot of twenty-two-year-olds seen at racquet-ball clubs
or singles bars or pleasure-boat marinas look pretty
much alike to the unpracticed eye. The item in the two
papers said little about George Mercer IV beyond giving
his physical description, but not many people in Savannah needed to be told who he was. The Mercers have
long been a prominent family in Savannah — a city
particularly conscious of prominent families. In Atlanta, a successful businessman who wants to upgrade

his background beyond simply awarding posthumous commissions to a few Civil War ancestors may allow his neighbors to infer that his family was originally from Savannah, Georgia's first settlement. The Mercers are the sort of family he would be trying to suggest — the sort of family whose discussions of military forebears tend to focus not on the Civil War but on the American Revolution. The Mercers are among the families that people in Savannah sometimes allow themselves to refer to as "the bluebloods" — a phrase that would be difficult to utter without a smile in Atlanta. Bluebloods still have enough power to be taken seriously in Savannah partly because Savannah has been the sort of place that respects their credentials, partly because Savannah has not been the kind of place that attracts a lot of ambitious newcomers who might shoulder them aside. Until their family company, which manufactured Great Dane truck trailers, was bought up by a conglomerate several years ago, the Mercers were one of Savannah's major industrial employers. George Mercer III, who did not remain with Great Dane after the purchase, is the chairman of the board of Savannah's Memorial Hospital and a former member of the Chatham County Commission. Although no one named Mercer is a force in the business life of Savannah these days, the Mercers remain the Mercers — stalwarts of the Oglethorpe Club, the kind of family that can ordinarily sort out any difficulty with a telephone call. It could be assumed by readers of the *Savannah Morning News* and *Evening Press* that the police would spare no effort in trying to find George Mercer IV. As it happened, there was another agency interested in the search for George Mercer IV — the Federal Bureau of Investigation. The F.B.I. had reason to believe that he had been kidnapped.

On River Street, where bars and restaurants have opened in restored warehouses in the past several years, F.B.I. agents were already showing bartenders a photograph of George Mercer IV. The people George Mercer IV went around with often ended up on River Street late in the evening — sometimes early in the evening. "They have a lot of time on their hands," someone who knows them said recently. Some of Mercer's friends were from his childhood — people who had gone to the same private schools and the same débutante parties — and some were just the people a single young man might meet over a pitcher of beer on River Street or at a party after a rugby match or during the quiet exchange of marijuana that young men with time on their hands think of as routine these days. The time they put in on River Street — or in similar bars near Armstrong State College, on the south side of Savannah — was not a matter of respite from working their way up in their chosen fields. Most of them had not got around to choosing a field. They tended to be young men who had put in a semester of college here and a semester of college there, but not enough semesters to have reached the point of selecting a major. Even those who still had recourse to the family's refrigerator or its speedboats needed spending money, but the jobs they took to get it tended to be temporary or seasonal or part time. Their ambitions for the future often seemed to settle on schemes for getting rich rather quickly, perhaps through being on the ground floor of some technological breakthrough in communications. For a while, George Mercer IV and a childhood friend talked of opening a video-disc outlet in Atlanta. They also talked about obtaining the Southeast regional franchise for a new electronic method of producing advertising spots.

George Mercer IV had a lot of enthusiasm for the schemes. His friends thought of him as rather gullible. He had been slow in school, with learning problems that included dyslexia. Once, when he was putting in a semester or so at LaGrange College, someone matched up the information that he liked to compose songs on the guitar with the information that his great-uncle was the songwriter Johnny Mercer, and the publicity resulted in the scheduling of a couple of public appearances. At the last minute, though, Mercer withdrew. He had decided he wasn't ready. His father diagnosed the problem as the sort of preperformance nervousness he calls "buck fever." After LaGrange, Mercer tended to play the guitar in public only when there were just four or five people left at the party. He spent some time at Armstrong State and at the night school of the University of Georgia, in Athens. Toward the end of 1979, while back in Savannah living with his parents, he got a job selling vacuum cleaners. It may not have appeared to be an appropriate job for a Mercer, but, as it happened, George Mercer IV seemed to enjoy selling vacuum cleaners. Some of his friends thought that the job had done a lot for George's self-confidence. His father agreed. He was hoping that sooner or later George Mercer IV might move from selling vacuum cleaners to selling Great Dane trailers. Then George Mercer IV disappeared.

Demands for ransom came almost immediately. There were notes. There were telephone calls. The instructions tended to be complicated, even bizarre. George Mercer III was instructed to draw a circle in orange spray paint at a certain intersection to indicate his coöperation. There were instructions to take the ransom — forty-two thousand dollars — in a small motorboat down the Ogeechee River, flying a flag with a yellow triangle sewn onto a field of green. At one point, the ransom was actually left in a wooded area, but nobody picked it up. When the item reporting George Mercer IV missing appeared in the *Savannah Morning News* and *Evening Press*, F.B.I. agents did not even know whether he was dead or alive — but they did have a pretty good hunch about who might have written the extortion notes. When they walked up and down River Street showing George Mercer's picture, they also carried with them a picture of Michael Harper.

Nobody has ever described Michael Harper as slow or gullible. "He could put anything over on anybody he wanted to," someone who knew him told the investigators. A slim, bearded young man about the age of

George Mercer IV, Harper had grown up in a suburb of Savannah, the son of a certified public accountant. He didn't have as many semesters of college as Mercer had, but people he came in contact with regularly described him as brilliant and accomplished — a wizard with electronics and math and computers, an expert at scuba diving and flying airplanes, a talker so glib that he had worked as a disc jockey when barely out of high school. They also described him as somewhat mysterious. No one seemed to know precisely where he lived. The jobs he mentioned holding ran from assistant manager of a fast-food chicken outlet to operator of what he described as a hush-hush project at Hunter Army Air Field called Quest Laboratories. The get-rich-quick schemes he discussed with friends were more complicated than opening a video-disc outlet — shadowy mail-order deals, for instance, and a plan to use a Savannah Police Department badge to hoodwink a couple of dope dealers out of some marijuana. One of Harper's schemes landed him in jail. In 1974, when he was only seventeen, he had been sentenced to fourteen months for trying to extort forty-five hundred dollars from a former neighbor by threatening to kill the man and his entire family. Later, in Augusta, he was convicted of theft by deception and given a probated sentence. Roger McLaughlin, one of the F.B.I. agents assigned to the Mercer kidnapping, had worked on the 1974 extortion case, and he thought he recognized Harper's style. Within a couple of days, the F.B.I. had ascertained that Harper had moved back

to Savannah from Augusta and that he knew George
Mercer IV. They had met at a rugby match.

One of the people who happened to be sitting at
the bar of Spanky's, on River Street, when the F.B.I.
showed the bartender pictures of George Mercer IV
and Michael Harper was Richard Sommers, an ebullient
young man who constitutes the photography staff of a
weekly Savannah newspaper called the *Georgia Gazette*. The *Gazette* was founded two and a half years
ago by a young man named Albert Scardino and his
wife, Marjorie, a lawyer who serves as publisher and
occasional typesetter. Albert Scardino, who has a graduate degree in journalism from the University of California, had tried free-lance writing for a while, and
had worked for the Associated Press in West Virginia,
and had produced a film on the coastal islands of
Georgia which was shown on the Public Broadcasting
System. For a while, he had tried to raise money —
from George Mercer III, among others — for a series
of films on wilderness areas around the world. Aside
from the journalistic experience he had picked up,
Scardino had another qualification for being the founding editor of a weekly newspaper in Savannah —
serious Savannah credentials. His father — a urologist
named Peter Scardino, who came to Savannah soon
after the Second World War — is not merely a prominent doctor but someone widely respected as a leading
force in improving the medical standards of the community. Dr. Scardino is not interested in Colonial

genealogy — he is quick to say that the only revolution his ancestors might have fought in was the one led by Garibaldi — and he is not the sort of man who would spend much time at any club not organized around the subject of urology. Still, his badges of acceptance in Savannah include membership in the Oglethorpe Club. For years, he and his wife have served on some of the same committees the Mercers serve on and have attended some of the same parties the Mercers attended. One of Albert Scardino's younger brothers grew up with George Mercer IV.

Although a lot of the weekly newspapers that have sprung up in the past decade seem designed specifically for the editors' contemporaries — or for some mythical twenty-nine-year-old purchaser of stereo equipment — the *Georgia Gazette* was founded to appeal to a general readership basically defined by its dissatisfaction with the commonly owned *Savannah Morning News* and *Evening Press*. In Savannah, the *News-Press* is widely described as innocuous or undistinguished; a contemporary of Albert Scardino is more likely to refer to it as "a Mickey Mouse operation." Albert and Marjorie Scardino hoped that after a few years of weekly publication the *Gazette* might gradually increase its frequency until it became a daily alternative to the *News-Press*. From the start, the *Gazette* did not grow at the pace the Scardinos had envisioned. Capital was a problem. They did manage one business coup, though, which promised to buy them some time for building advertising and circulation: in January 1979 the *Ga-*

zette replaced the *Evening Press* as what is known in Georgia as the sheriff's gazette — the newspaper designated to carry the advertisements that lawyers in the county place to satisfy requirements of public notice. The sheriff, one of the three county officials empowered to decide which paper is designated, had persuaded a probate judge to go along with a switch to the *Gazette* — either because the sheriff was impressed by Albert Scardino's arguments about the benefits of encouraging competition or because, as people around the courthouse say, he was irritated at the *Evening Press*. The designation meant thousands of dollars a year in automatic advertising, and the advertising meant a subscription from every lawyer in the county, and the readership of lawyers meant one more sales point to potential advertisers. The *Georgia Gazette* is not the sort of alternative weekly in which official advertisements seem incongruous. It carries conventional business and social news, as well as some pieces that might offend potential advertisers and investors. It has never been known for sensationalism or scatology. Albert Scardino comes to work in a coat and tie. The *Gazette* had obviously taken some care to recognize the value that Savannah places on being respectable — which is why people in Savannah were astounded when Albert Scardino, against the wishes of the Mercer family, published a front-page story on February 11th revealing that George Mercer IV was not merely missing but presumed kidnapped, and that Michael Harper was the chief suspect.

Although the F.B.I. agent at Spanky's had not said why he wanted to know if anybody had seen George Mercer IV or Michael Harper, Richard Sommers could think of only two reasons for the F.B.I. to be involved — a large drug bust or a kidnapping. Sommers had started questioning some of Mercer's friends, and Scardino had bluffed a lot of the rest of the story out of a local police official. Although George Mercer III would not admit that his son had been kidnapped, it was clear that he did not want a story printed. "In the tried-and-true Savannah tradition, he called one of our stockholders," Scardino said later. It was argued, by the stockholder and others, that a story might endanger George Mercer IV if he really had been kidnapped. Albert Scardino was not persuaded. Mercer had been missing for ten days. The F.B.I. was openly looking for him. When Scardino pressed an agent at the Savannah F.B.I. office to say whether a story might be harmful, the agent would only repeat F.B.I. policy about not commenting on a case in progress. Scardino says he could not see the sort of clear and present danger that would have caused him to go along with, say, the embargo on stories about the American Embassy employees hiding in the Canadian Embassy in Teheran. He telephoned George Mercer III to inform him that the story would be printed and to suggest that the Mercers make some preparation for the press interest that would follow — preparations such as designating a spokesman. The man Albert Scardino was dealing with, after all, was practically a friend of the family. George

Mercer III said, as Scardino recalls it, "You'd better quit worrying about a couple of little birds and streams and start worrying about the value of human life."

A lot of people in Savannah thought that Albert Scardino made a mistake in printing the story. They thought that whatever he had learned in journalism school about the people's right to know simply did not apply. Some people thought that Scardino was just trying to make a splash. Some people thought the story might endanger young George Mercer's life. Some people were pretty certain it would endanger Albert Scardino's newspaper. They were amazed that Scardino, whose background had obviously enabled him to understand how the city worked, could have suddenly chosen a course that was so patently self-destructive. The Mercers and those close to them were furious. The Trust Company of Georgia, where people like the Mercers have always done their banking, cancelled a large advertising campaign that was about to begin in the *Gazette*. Twenty people wrote angry letters to the editor cancelling their subscriptions. Some people pointedly snubbed Albert Scardino on the street. One aunt of George Mercer IV ended an angry telephone conversation with Marjorie Scardino late one night by saying that she hoped the Scardino children would be kidnapped. Albert Scardino heard that a regular subject of conversation at one luncheon table at the Oglethorpe Club was how to put the *Georgia Gazette* out of business.

Some people claimed that the *Gazette* story, aside

from any danger it might pose for George Mercer IV, would warn Michael Harper to get out of town, and they may have been right: on the day the story was published, Harper left Savannah. He had the bad luck, though, to hitch a ride with a van that was stopped for speeding. Within a day, he was back in jail — held for a probation violation — and the F.B.I. started amassing enough evidence to charge him with trying to extort forty-two thousand dollars from George Mercer III. Harper admitted nothing. He did say that if the police would let him out of jail he would help look for Mercer — probably in Greenville, South Carolina. Finally, toward the end of April, the police found Mercer themselves — buried in a shallow grave in the woods on the grounds of Armstrong State. He had been shot twice. Michael Harper was charged with murder.

The coroner said that George Mercer IV had probably been killed the first day he was missing. The implication that the *Gazette* story had appeared well after Mercer's death did not do much to reduce animosity toward Albert Scardino. "The real improper thing," Scardino has said, "was not that we endangered his life but that an upstanding, powerful, rich member of the community asked us to do something and we ignored his request." A lot of people in Savannah would probably agree that there was something in the Mercers' anger beyond the genuine concern that any family would have for the safety of a son. Albert Scardino believes that people close to the Mercers were furious not simply because they had been defied but because they had been defied by someone whose family had been accepted into the group of people in Savannah accustomed to sorting out any difficulty with a telephone call. "That was the special betrayal that caused the special animosity," he says. Richard Sommers, who did not grow up with the Mercers and the Scardinos, has a different way of explaining the special animosity. "They didn't consider the crime a crime against society but a crime against them," he said recently. "They wanted it handled their way. We treated it as a crime against society. We made them common."

In July, Albert Scardino learned that at the end of 1980 the legal advertising that had been given to the *Gazette* a year and a half before would revert to the *Evening Press* — cutting the *Gazette*'s annual income by some thirty per cent. The official who pushed for the reversion was the same sheriff who had been the *Gazette*'s champion. For a year and a half, of course, the *Evening Press* had been trying to win back the advertising, using every form of pressure at its disposal; the officials in charge of the designation were even lobbied by *News-Press* reporters assigned to cover their activities. Last spring, though, the officials began to receive telephone calls from what one of them has called "surprisingly high places." George Mercer III says he had no part in a campaign to deprive the *Gazette* of legal advertising, but he also acknowledges that he had heard about the telephone calls — made, perhaps, by people he describes as "misguidedly thinking they were representing me." There are, as Mercer suggests, a number of other ways that the reversion can be explained. For a while, Scardino himself had an ornate theory involving the Georgia senatorial election. It may even be, of course, that the sheriff simply changed his mind for sound reasons of public policy — although that interpretation is not bolstered by his refusal to discuss the matter. Albert Scardino now believes that the change was brought about by a combination of factors, but he has become convinced that one of them was a decision made over lunch at the Oglethorpe Club.

This winter, Michael Harper finally went on trial. Just before the trial started, he pleaded guilty to extortion, but he still contended that George Mercer IV had been alive the last time he saw him. According to his defense on the murder charge — revealed by the *Georgia Gazette* just before the trial got under way — everything had flowed from an attempt that he and George Mercer IV made to raise capital for a business they wanted to launch: a custom-stereo-speaker concern called Quest Labs. Harper said that he and Mercer and two other people, whom he refused to name, had tried to raise the capital by buying more than forty thousand dollars' worth of marijuana for resale. They had bought the marijuana on credit, Harper said, but it had been stolen before they could resell it. Under threat of death from the people who wanted their forty-two thousand, the four partners had decided to extort the money from George Mercer's father — with young George himself as a full participant. When the extortion scheme fell apart, Harper said, the four had fled in different directions. Harper calmly, sometimes brilliantly, defended his story on the witness stand. The jury took four hours to convict him of murder. He was sentenced to life imprisonment. Maintaining his innocence to the end, Harper said he could only offer condolences to the Mercer family on George's death. "He was a friend of mine," Harper said.

Not many people in Savannah believed Harper's story. It sounded like a knock-off of the defense in the Bronfman kidnapping. Still, there are a lot of people who don't believe that, as the prosecution maintained, Michael Harper simply kidnapped George Mercer IV and shot him in cold blood to avoid having a prisoner to guard while negotiating the ransom. The *Gazette* coverage has constantly pointed out loose ends in that version of what happened. There are other stories floating around Savannah to explain what might have happened between George Mercer IV, the gullible son of a rich family, and the brilliant but twisted Michael Harper. A lot of them, like a lot of stories that try to explain mysteries these days, have to do with drugs. What makes some people in Savannah feel vulnerable is that George Mercer IV and Michael Harper knew each other at all. George Mercer III still finds it astonishing that the young people Michael Harper came in contact with didn't know or didn't care about his criminal record. Thinking about it recently, a resident of

Savannah in his sixties said, "What this business with drugs and the new life style and all that has changed is this: We didn't use to have to worry about our kids' mingling with someone like that."

After a short period of coolness, people close to the Mercers began to treat Dr. Peter Scardino and his wife the way they had treated them before George Mercer IV disappeared. George Mercer III is quick to express his respect for Dr. Scardino. The Scardinos were quick to express their sympathy to the Mercers. Whatever might have been done by relatives of the Mercers, Dr. Scardino has never thought of the Mercers themselves as the sort of people who could tell a mother that they hoped her children would be kidnapped. A few days after the trial, George Mercer III said, "I'm too drained spiritually and mentally and physically to have any animosity toward anybody," but he couldn't speak of Albert Scardino without the animosity's coming to the surface. The family's bitterness toward Scardino had been increased, in fact, by the *Gazette*'s coverage of the trial, which Mercer considered a matter of "gross callousness and insensitivity." Despite prosecution testimony to the contrary, the *Gazette* wrote, investigators had been told that George Mercer IV did some minor dealing in marijuana and perhaps cocaine. Even the *News-Press,* whose coverage of the case had been dominated by politesse (a February feature about George Mercer IV and his friends had been headlined "MERCER CALLED 'TYPICAL' YOUNG MAN"), had been forced to bring up the subject of drugs in covering Michael Harper's defense. A day after the sentencing, the Mercers, who had been dealing with the press through a family spokesman, asked a local television reporter they knew to come to their house with a film crew. Mrs. Mercer read a statement saying that their son had not been involved in drugs and could not have been involved in any schemes with Michael Harper. After she had read the statement, Mrs. Mercer added, "I would like to say that George was not a friend of this man."

The Mystery of
Walter Bopp

Tucson, Arizona
May 1981

WHAT HAPPENED to Walter Bopp is a mystery. In
fact, the more that is known about what happened to
him, the more mysterious it becomes. The first incident
did not seem mysterious at all. In the fall of 1979,
Walter Bopp, a vigorous man in his late seventies, was
attacked and presumably robbed in downtown Tucson
— right in front of the business he and his wife had
founded in 1934 as the first health-food store in the
city. The incident did not make the newspapers. Tucson is one of those middle-sized Sun Belt cities that are
becoming accustomed to the routine muggings and bur-
glaries which a few years ago were associated with the
huge old industrial cities of the Northeast. It is no
longer unusual for residents of Tucson to own a sophisticated burglar-alarm system or a gun or even, as
Walter Bopp did, an attack dog. The second incident
— a house fire last spring which the fire department

blamed on an electrical short circuit — would probably have gone unreported as well except that when
firemen reached the cellar they found, to their under-
standable dismay, a supply of dynamite and blasting
caps that, according to a department spokesman, could
have caused a large enough explosion to obliterate
Bopp's house, all the firemen in it, and a couple of
neighboring houses. The mystery of why someone
would store dynamite in his basement seemed to be
cleared up when Bopp explained that it was from a
nonproducing mine he had operated near Arivaca — a
tiny gold- and silver-mining town about an hour in the
direction of the Mexican border. Last December,
though, Bopp was involved in an incident that was not
simply mysterious in itself but suffused the previous
incidents with mystery. On a Saturday morning, someone phoned Bopp's second store, on East Speedway
Boulevard, and informed a clerk that the proprietor
had met with an accident and could be found in the
back storeroom. Walter Bopp had been bound with tape
and badly beaten the night before. He had serious facial
bruises and several broken ribs and a broken pelvis.
His attack dog had been killed by having its belly slit
open. His pickup truck had been driven to the downtown store and then set on fire. Both stores had been
gone through, but no money was missing.

Bopp claimed that all the incidents were related —
that the fire had been caused by arson rather than a
short circuit, that the mugging a year earlier had been
not a simple mugging but an act of terrorism. He even

implied that he knew who was to blame — but that was as far as he would go in helping police identify his tormentors. He wouldn't say who and he wouldn't say why. "It's the same people," he was quoted as telling his interrogators. "I don't want to say anything more." Two weeks later, just after Bopp was released from the hospital, it was reported that someone had backed a truck up to his Speedway store and was presumably loading something into it while colleagues stood by with what looked like machine guns or automatic rifles. The police arrived too late, and if Walter Bopp knew who might be removing what from his store he wasn't saying. He still hadn't said in January, when he reëntered the hospital and, a day or two later, died of a pulmonary embolism. All of which set a lot of people in Tucson thinking about what in the world might have happened to Walter Bopp.

"I didn't think he had an enemy in the world," one of Walter Bopp's employees had told the *Arizona Daily Star* after the December beating. That is, of course, a remark often made when a respectable citizen meets with what is obviously not random violence. To the casual customer of Bopp Health Food, Walter Bopp probably did appear to be a particularly unlikely candidate for vicious assault — a robust, rosy-cheeked old vegetarian whose knowledge of herbal remedies led some of his customers to refer to him as Dr. Bopp. A Swiss immigrant who retained a slight accent, Bopp was known as a man who worked hard and lived frugally. A lot of people in Tucson had seen him on the back of his pickup truck loading or unloading stock; nobody in Tucson had ever seen him in a necktie. Who would want to terrorize a simple purveyor of wheat germ and herbal tea?

It wasn't long, of course, before it became known that Bopp had interests beyond health food. The *Star* reported in January that he had been in disagreements with several people about land near Arivaca. It also reported that he had been in "supernatural" activities. Then two young reporters for the *Tucson Citizen*, Dan Huff and Shawn Hubler, poked around in Walter Bopp's life and found people who referred to him not as Dr. Bopp but as Dr. Jekyll and Mr. Hyde. Bopp, the *Citizen* reporters discovered, had indeed been capable of great kindness. He had also been, they wrote, a "tight-lipped, sometimes hateful man who believed in witches and who once said that Lyndon Johnson, Lady Bird and Robert McNamara turned into animals and slithered over White House fences at night." It was known in Tucson that Bopp had divorced his wife a few years earlier, after forty-seven years of marriage, but the *Citizen* piece revealed that he was thought to have done so under advice from a psychic. (Most of Bopp's acquaintances — he didn't seem to have any close friends — were unaware that he had remarried until the newspapers carried the name of a second wife as his survivor.) It also revealed that Bopp had strong racist views about Mexicans and blacks. The kindly Dr. Bopp, Huff and Hubler were told, had been a contentious man who never admitted he was wrong and never let loose of a grudge.

Newspaper reports indicating that there were areas in Bopp's life which could indeed have produced an enemy or two did not clear up the mystery, of course; they simply made it more complicated. Had Walter Bopp been terrorized because of a dispute over a silver claim? Could he have discovered something in Arivaca that someone else wanted to know? Was it possible that he had found himself among the sort of cultists who beat up elderly vegetarians? What were Bopp's tormentors after? Gold? Silver? Information? His store? What could have been secret or private enough to restrain Walter Bopp from helping police find the people who had left him bound and beaten on the floor of his storeroom?

From the start, of course, there were ways of explaining what happened to Walter Bopp that did not require knowledge of his ventures into mining or racial theory or the supernatural. Who leans on respectable businessmen? "They were obviously hit men," a clerk at Bopp's store said after the December beating. Tucson happens to have a substantial and well-publicized colony of the sort of citizens who are photographed by the F.B.I. at funerals, and a lot of speculation naturally centered on the possibility that Bopp had run afoul of the mob. Did Walter Bopp have something the mob wanted? Were mobsters trying to persuade him to do something they wanted? It was also possible, of course, that Walter Bopp had simply wandered into some private dispute over pride or sex or vengeance. People in Tucson developed a stunning variety of theories to account for what happened to him: he was a loan shark, he was a bagman, he was a drug dealer, he was an arms dealer, he was a rich miser. "I know he was sitting on a lot of gold," a bartender at the Poco Loco, a tavern next door to Bopp's Speedway store, said not long ago. "He had been buying gold that'd be worth a million dollars in today's market. I think that's why he was dusted."

Walter Bopp arrived in America in the twenties and, doing farm work, made his way across the country to California. Just before the crash of 1929, he sent for his childhood sweetheart — a young Englishwoman who had been at a Swiss school in Bopp's village. Apparently, whatever money he had saved was lost in a get-rich-quick real-estate scheme; at the beginning of the Depression he was working as a dishwasher. What brought him to Tucson in the early thirties was a job as a salad chef at the Pioneer Hotel. When Bopp Health Food opened in 1934, in a tiny downtown storefront, Bopp's wife, Mae, used to say that the cash register was worth more than the stock. Bopp let his wife mind the store for a couple of years while he held on to his salad-chef job. Then they both began working — working without taking vacations or weekends, as far as anyone in Tucson remembers — to build what was for a dozen years the only health-food business in Tucson.

Health food was hardly a national fad in the thirties. "It was not just unfashionable," someone who got into the business a decade or so later said recently. "It was practically clandestine." Tucson, though, did have more than its share of potential customers. In those days, doctors used to send patients to the Arizona desert on the theory that the dry air would alleviate suffering from allergies or asthma or arthritis or emphysema — or simply on the theory that it might be a soothing climate for someone whose disease seemed beyond the reach of conventional medicine. Some of the desperately ill looked for remedies in nutrition, and Walter Bopp was their adviser. He also developed a trade supplying grain and cereal in bulk to ranchers. As a businessman, Walter Bopp was Old World — thrifty, hardworking, cautious, impervious to suggestions about merchandising techniques. He didn't hold much with spring sales or regular salary increases. The original store remained the same size, in a part of downtown that gradually became characterized by cheap furniture stores and pawnshops. Bopp didn't open a second store until the sixties — on East Speedway Boulevard, a wide street that for miles seems to be one run-on strip-shopping development. The Speedway store was modern when Bopp built it, but hardly modern compared with the flashy health-food chains that blossomed when the business began to attract people who saw health food as a market rather than a cause. Walter Bopp plugged away — grumbling about the insincere people who had come into the business, moving supplies from one store to the other in his pickup truck, working late into the night on his order forms. The block he had chosen on Speedway turned out to be even less uplifting than the old block downtown. After a while, Bopp found himself with the Poco Loco on one side and on the other a place called the Empress Theatre, which offered hard-core films, "adult books and novelties," and a "hot-tub spa." Bopp complained belligerently about tavern and porn-store customers jamming the parking spaces in front of his shop and using the small parking lot he had for his own customers. "An American businessman might have just moved," someone who knew him at that time said recently. "But he was very set in his ways."

Bopp's ways were strange from the start. Mae Bopp — a diminutive, well-spoken woman who seemed almost timid, particularly in his presence — worked constantly in the store, but the Bopps were otherwise not seen together. He seemed to live mainly in the back of the downtown store. He was kind to some employees and cold to others. He fired at least two clerks in the belief that they were witches who were trying to hex him. ("He was good to me until then," one of them has said. "He was a sweet old man.") To a lot of people, he seemed secretive and aloof. His feelings against Jews were even more vitriolic than his feelings against blacks and Mexicans. Some people who knew Bopp for years were unaware of his racial views; some were treated to them in intense, sotto-voce lectures in a back corner of the store. "He was very intelligent," one of his former employees said recently. "He knew herbs very well. He was the first one to help you if you went to him with a problem. He had so many good ways —

it's too bad he got mixed up in all that weird stuff. He said some weird things about Jewish people. Once, he told me that a customer was a witch and I shouldn't look her in the eye. He'd start talking real mysterious, real low. He told me she would come to my bedroom in the form of a vampire, and I should get a silver cross to ward her off. I don't believe in witches, but, I'll tell you, when he got through with me I wished I had a silver cross."

Among his other views, Bopp had a strong belief that the economic system — or perhaps all of society — would come crashing down one day, in an even more disastrous way than it had come crashing down in 1929. At that point, of course, stocks and real estate and even paper money would not be worth having. The only wealth would be in gold and silver. There is reason to believe that Walter Bopp did indeed have some gold or silver stashed somewhere. Gold and silver would allow him to survive the economic disaster. According to someone who used to work for Bopp, the silver would have an even more important use: "He figured he could use the silver against Satan. Evil spirits are afraid of silver."

As a young man in southern California, Bopp had shopped around in what must have been the Western world's most extensive display of yogis and mystics and cults, eventually settling on a Hindu offshoot called the Benares League. His belief in the occult may have intensified as he grew older. He seemed more certain of the forces allied against him. He told an acquaintance that he had paid to have a counter-hex placed on someone who was trying to hex him. The woman he married a few months before his death is said to be a soothsayer or a psychic — the same one who advised him during the dissolution of his previous marriage. A former employee of Bopp's was told by the police that the closest Bopp would come to identifying his assailants was to say that he had been done in by the Evil Force. A lot of people who knew Bopp remain convinced that his death had something to do with his otherworldly beliefs. ("It must have been that damn cult thing.") But what? A hex does not in fact cause a vicious beating. The secrets of the afterlife are not ordinarily sought by torturing a man of spiritual powers until he tells. How can Bopp's silence be explained? Could Walter Bopp — confused, increasingly obsessed with the otherworldly, slipping toward paranoia — have mistaken a couple of thugs after gold for the Evil Force?

The most romantic notions of what might have happened to Walter Bopp have to do with mining, which has been part of the folklore of southern Arizona for much longer than the mob has. A lot of people in Tucson who may do something else for a living prospect as a sort of sideline — somewhere between a hobby and a disease — and for at least thirty years Walter Bopp was one of them. Some of them still dream of the big strike — a lode of silver that has somehow been missed by all the holes poked into the desert all of these years, the fabulous lost mines that the Jesuits are said to have left when they were expelled from Arizona in the eighteenth century. Some people in Tucson theorized that Walter Bopp might have hit such a strike, but the mining people around Arivaca find that notion amusing. From what they say, Bopp must have been one of the most consistently unsuccessful miners in the state.

"I don't think he ever shipped a pound of ore out of here," someone familiar with mining in Arivaca said recently. Occasionally, Bopp would show up at the assay office with a test bore that looked mildly promising, but, as far as anyone knows, he never followed it up. Bopp was not simply a weekend prospector with a pan or a pickaxe. He filed dozens of claims and did dozens of test bores. ("He sank holes all over this country.") Just outside of Arivaca, he kept a couple of miners working for a dozen years to sink two shafts deep into the ground. There are people in Arivaca who believe that Bopp was almost willfully unsuccessful — ignoring promising samples, choosing the least likely place to drill. His method of finding gold or silver was what prospectors call "witchin' it" — trying to divine it, the way a dowser divines water. It is not uncommon for prospectors — even prospectors who don't believe in witches — to try to witch gold or silver, and apparently just about all of them do better at it than Walter Bopp did.

People around Arivaca remember Bopp as a contentious man — quick to assert his rights, quick to take an argument to court. It is possible, of course, that he got into a dispute with someone over a claim or had some mine information someone else wanted or let one of the arguments miners are always having with ranchers in southern Arizona get out of hand. Nobody who knows much about mining thinks that explains what happened to him. They don't think that Bopp got into a dispute of great seriousness, and they don't think what happened to him is characteristic of the way such a dispute would be settled. That doesn't mean that they think there was nothing mysterious about Walter Bopp's mining operations. They wonder where he got all of the money he spent for what miners call "holes in the ground." A lot of them figure he was using someone else's money. Whose? What does that have to do with what happened to Walter Bopp?

The police have been to Arivaca and they have visited one of the people Bopp suspected of witchcraft, but they are apparently not taken with some of the more ornate theories about the fate of Walter Bopp. Detectives, in the accepted manner, appear to have concentrated their attention on those closest to Walter Bopp and on those who might profit from his death and on anyone who both knew him and seems capable of having terrorized him. (One of Bopp's Speedway neighbors, for example, was once charged with extortion and, in plea bargaining, pleaded guilty to aggravated assault.) It has been five months now since Walter Bopp was attacked, and there is some feeling in Tucson that the police have shifted their energies to other matters. The mystery may always be a mystery.

Among people familiar with the case, of course, the speculation continues. Someone has called Dan Huff at the *Citizen* with an involved story based on Bopp's being connected with Swiss banking houses. Someone else reported having seen Bopp at a Klan recruiting meeting. The various aspects of Bopp's life can be put together in any number of combinations: Bopp owed the mob money he had borrowed to pour into holes in the ground around Arivaca; Bopp met some hippie cultists in the desert — where hippies still seem to exist, as if preserved by the dry climate — and made the mistake of telling them that he had a fortune in gold; Bopp's views on race led him into contact with some people whose viciousness went beyond sotto-voce lectures; Bopp was using mob money for mining; Bopp was using Swiss banking money for mining; Bopp was using Fascist money for mining.

It is said around Tucson that Bopp's widow intends to reopen the health-food stores, but it is also said that the East Speedway store has been sold to the porno operation next door. Both stores are locked, with ornamental grilles protecting their windows. At the Speedway store, the grille is festooned with signs saying that parking is for customers of Bopp Health Food only. In the window, among the displays of sweet orange-spice tea and the Naturade jojoba hair-treatment formula, is a handwritten note that says, "Closed due to death in family."

A Father-Son Operation

Grundy County, Iowa
September 1982

THE SOIL in Grundy County is often spoken of as the
richest soil in Iowa — which means, Grundy County
residents sometimes add, that it must be about the
richest soil in the world. "The land is mostly a gentle,
undulating prairie with just sufficient slope to thoroughly drain it," somebody wrote of Grundy County
farmland in 1860. "There is not the same area in the
state with less wasteland. . . . The soil is black mould
of the prairie, deep and strong for all kinds of crops."
Although the farmers who come in to Grundy Center,
the county seat, to do their banking and buy their supplies manage to find plenty about the weather that is
worthy of complaint, crop failures in Grundy County
are even rarer than armed robberies. "Oh, we get six
or seven crop failures a year," a local resident said
recently over morning coffee at Manly's drugstore, on
the main street of Grundy Center. "But they're all in
the bar or the drugstore." Agribusiness spokesmen who
routinely talk about the American family farm in the

past tense are apparently not familiar with Grundy
County. All its farms are family farms. Many of them
are owned by the same families that carved them out
of the prairie in the last decades of the nineteenth
century. In those days, the northern part of the county
was virtually all German — it was settled by serious,
hardworking farm people from East Friesland, near
the Dutch border — and it is virtually all German
today. The family names are the same. People in
Grundy Center still like to say that you can walk from
a point just a couple of miles north of the county
courthouse to Parkersburg, fifteen miles away, and almost never be off land that is owned by one member
of the Meester clan or another. In some ways, the lives
of the Grundy County Germans have not changed a
lot since the days when walking was about the only
way to make the trip. It is true, of course, that they
now own sixty-thousand-dollar tractors and that they
routinely drive twenty-five miles to a shopping mall in
Cedar Falls for their groceries and that many of them
can easily afford to fly to Germany to visit the villages
of their forebears. It is also true, though, that they remain serious, hardworking farm people. Most of them
still lead lives that revolve tightly around their families
and their land. On Sundays, they go to church — to
small country Reformed churches on county blacktops
or to conservative versions of Presbyterian or Baptist
churches in nearby trading towns like Parkersburg and
Aplington. The Sabbath is still taken seriously as a day
of rest in northern Grundy County; not many people

would mow their lawn or wash their car or repair the
roof of their barn on a Sunday afternoon — not within
sight of the road, at least. Many people still live in the
rambling white farmhouses that their forebears built
on the family's original plot of land — what farm people in Iowa still call the home place. The houses stand
surrounded by huge groves of shade trees that are visible for miles across an otherwise almost treeless prairie.
In all directions, the black Iowa soil is planted in corn
and soybeans. In Grundy County, a good farmer can
expect a yield of a hundred and fifty bushels of corn
an acre, and it is taken for granted that just about all
farmers in Grundy County are good farmers. One of
the best — one of the best, that is, until his life began
to change in ways that his neighbors still can't quite
explain — was a man named Lawrence Hartman.

Four or five years ago, when Lawrence Hartman was
in his middle fifties, there didn't seem to be much of
what life in Grundy County could offer that he didn't
have. He owned one of the most prosperous corn-and-
bean farms in the county. He ran a large cattle-feeding
operation. He had served as a trustee of his township
and a trustee of the Presbyterian Church and a member of the Landfill Commission and a member of the
Election Board and a member of the Condemnation
Board. His wife, Esther, was a Meester — a member of the largest and most prominent of northern
Grundy County's founding families. His two grown
sons, Rodney and Rollyn, worked with him on the
Hartman land, as he had worked with his own father.

Rodney, who was then about thirty, was a big, beefy, occasionally rambunctious bachelor who was gradually settling back down to life in Grundy County after a couple of years at a business college in Waterloo and a particularly unsettling year as a combat infantryman in Vietnam. Rollyn, eight years younger, was a quieter man, who had only recently left home for the first time: he got married and moved to a farmhouse just down the road from his parents. When Rollyn was asked some time later to describe the sort of farming the Hartmans did, he summed it up in one sentence: "It's a father-son operation."

In farm families, where people who have ties of blood may also be connected as business partners, it is customary to be explicit about the terms of the partnership. When Lawrence Hartman's father retired and moved to town — in 1947, the year Lawrence and Esther Hartman were married — Lawrence began farming the Hartman home place, two hundred and forty acres on a county road known as the Buck Grove Blacktop, in a fifty-fifty partnership. He worked his father's land with his father's equipment for half the profits. Thirty years later, Lawrence Hartman's arrangement with his two sons was as clearly defined. Lawrence and Rollyn Hartman were fifty-fifty partners in a hog operation — the corn for feed provided by the father, the labor by the son. In the main farming operation, Rodney and Rollyn traded their labor — they prepared the ground, their father did the actual planting — for the use of Lawrence Hartman's machinery and his planting expertise on a smaller farm they had bought for themselves with his help. The one person whose labors in the family's enterprises seemed beyond any agreements or categories was Esther Hartman.

Esther Hartman seemed to have inherited undiluted the values brought to Iowa by the God-fearing, thrifty, hardworking settlers from East Friesland. She was strict about going to church and strict about keeping the Sabbath and strict about not having any liquor in her house. Although she was three years older than her husband, and had a slight hunch from curvature of the spine, she seemed to have the energy of a strapping farm girl. She kept an immaculate house. She canned vegetables long after most of her neighbors had been won over by the frozen-food cases of the Cedar Falls supermarkets. She baked pies and she baked cakes. In the Hartman household, it was taken for granted that Rodney, who lived nearby, would bring his laundry home to his mother every week. Esther Hartman had always done the laundry and the spring cleaning for her elder brothers — bachelor twins who together still farmed the Meester home place, a couple of miles away, speaking the Plattdeutsch of their childhood to each other over supper. From the beginning, she had worked alongside her husband on the Hartman farm — not just managing the house but opening gates and helping with the livestock and keeping the books.

After thirty years of hard work by the Hartman family, the books looked remarkably good. The Hartmans had most of their land paid off; their income was more than respectable, even by city standards. As a farmer, Lawrence Hartman was known as a good manager — a man who could get his land plowed and planted with less equipment and less labor than his neighbors required for the same number of acres, a man who could judge the best time to plant and the best time to buy supplies in quantity. He was also shrewd at acquiring property. The Hartman holdings grew steadily. Esther inherited some land from her family, but mostly Lawrence bought land from his neighbors. Several times in the late sixties, he bought nearby farms by first arranging to sell off what is known as the acreage — the house and the outbuildings and the few acres they stand on — and then using the money as down payment. About the most he paid for land was five or six hundred dollars an acre, and gradually it became clear that Grundy County farmland at that price was a great bargain. In the middle seventies, the value of farmland in Grundy County seemed to increase almost daily. The boom was not the result of outside speculation; local farmers were attempting to increase their holdings. They were trying to expand partly because of two or three particularly good crops in a row and partly because increasingly efficient and expensive farm machinery made it sensible to spread a huge investment in tractors and combines over an extra hundred or two hundred acres of land. There was another factor that people in Grundy County talk about now and then in the drugstore over morning coffee or in the tavern over a beer: for one reason or another, a lot of people had come to the realization at about the same time that the black soil of Grundy County was limited in supply, and that nobody was ever going to produce any more of it. Around 1977, prime farmland in Grundy County was changing hands for thirty-five hundred dollars an acre and going toward four thousand. Lawrence Hartman — a man whose education amounted to eight years in a county school, a man who had started with a half share in a quarter section, a man who had worked with his hands just about every day of every week except the Sabbath since childhood — had more than five hundred acres of it.

One evening in 1978, in a bar called the Apartment Lounge in Cedar Falls, Lawrence Hartman picked up a woman named Katherine Sunderman. The Apartment Lounge is in the College Square shopping center — a large, modern mall close to the campus of the University of Northern Iowa. Although the designer of the Apartment Lounge included examples of just about every type of decoration found in any type of American bar, from hanging plants to brewery art, the design element that seems most appropriate to the clientele is a series of drawings of Northern Iowa fraternity and sorority houses. At the Apartment Lounge, the waitresses are likely to be young women wearing crew-neck sweaters, and the bartender may be a physical-education major in a swim-team T-shirt. In that atmosphere, Katherine Sunderman, who worked as a cocktail waitress herself at one time or another, stood out — a divorcée in her early thirties with a lot of tight blond curls and a habit of calling all women "babe" and all men "tiger." The people who worked at the Apartment Lounge referred to her among themselves as Flo, after the brassy, gum-chewing waitress in a television sit-com. That night in 1978, she and a friend fell into conversation with a couple of men at the next table — Lawrence Hartman and a partner of his in a cattle-feeding operation. Not long after that, Katherine Sunderman and Lawrence Hartman were thought of by the Apartment Lounge staff as a couple — Flo and the quiet farmer.

Why was Lawrence Hartman trying to pick up a cocktail waitress over a drink in a Cedar Falls lounge instead of discussing the weather with his neighbors over coffee in Aplington or over a beer in Parkersburg? What had changed a family man and community leader of unassailable reputation? Some people in Grundy County would say simply "Cattle-buying." A corn-and-beans farmer never wanders far; he even comes home in the middle of the day for dinner. Someone who buys cattle — buys them with the thought of feeding them for a year and then selling them — may find himself in a large city with the day's work done and an empty evening on his hands. "It's almost like a travelling salesman," someone in a café in Aplington said recently. "You got to be pretty well grounded." For thirty years, Lawrence Hartman had in fact seemed pretty well grounded. There was a time when he managed to buy cattle by ordering over the phone from a dealer in Sioux City whom he knew and trusted, or by driving to Sioux City with Esther, so that she could go shopping with the dealer's wife while the deal was being made. By the time he met Katherine Sunderman at the Apartment Lounge, though, he had begun travelling to places like Kansas City to buy cattle, with some cattle-buyers who were known in Grundy County for being interested in big-city entertainment as well as in livestock. "He'd been here thirty-some years farming, and then he got to the city," Rodney Hartman said not long ago. In the city, according to an Aplington man who dealt with Lawrence Hartman for a number of years, "he had some money and he probably found it could buy him some goodies he hadn't been aware of." Lawrence Hartman began to pay less attention to the farm than he had in the past. He began talking about the pleasures of drinking Screwdrivers at cocktail lounges. Then, Rodney Hartman has said, "*she* came along."

Rodney and Rollyn Hartman found out who she was almost as soon as their mother finally told them that their father had apparently been seeing another woman for some time. They traced a number from a telephone bill to Katherine Sunderman's mobile home, in a trailer park outside a little town between Aplington and Cedar Falls. When Lawrence Hartman arrived home the next morning and spoke harshly to his wife, apparently not realizing that Rodney was in the house, Rodney hit him hard enough to break his jaw. Even now, Rodney finds it astonishing that he hit the man he had been brought up to respect and obey. "I was probably out of line bad," he said. "But I couldn't handle it." It was not the last violence to pass between father and sons. Once, Rollyn Hartman and his father exchanged blows. Once, Lawrence Hartman threatened Rollyn with a shotgun, and Rollyn tried to knock him down the stairs. Once, Rodney and Rollyn forcibly dragged Lawrence Hartman to the Happy Chef restaurant in Cedar Falls so that the sons could confront Katherine Sunderman as a home-wrecker in their father's presence.

Lawrence Hartman had told his sons that his personal life was none of their business, but they considered it literally their business. They were concerned not just about their mother but also about the future of the farm they had worked on all their lives. "My father lost his ability to manage," Rodney has said. Lawrence Hartman was often gone, even at the time of year when hogs had to be taken to market or planting was imminent. "We had to know what was going to be corn and what was going to be beans," Rollyn has said. "If you farm eight or nine hundred acres, you may have one chance at a crop. You'd better be there when the weather's right." At times, Lawrence said he wanted to work out his marital problems. There were sessions with a marriage counsellor and with the Hartmans' minister, Charles Orr. At times, Hartman assured his sons that he had given up Katherine Sunderman, only to disappear again over a long weekend. "We tried a lot of things," Rodney Hartman said recently. "But we never did get the job done." For two Christmases in a row, Lawrence Hartman was absent when his family

— his wife and his sons and his daughter-in-law and, the second year, his first grandchild — gathered at the Hartman home place. It was an act that seemed to shock them almost more than anything else he had done. What it all meant in Rollyn's view was that Lawrence Hartman was "no longer part of our family." In the spring of 1980, Esther Hartman, who had been raised in a society where the permanence of the marriage contract was unquestioned, finally began divorce proceedings. She got a court injunction that barred her husband from their farmhouse and severely limited the amount of money he could draw from the family account.

Within a couple of months, she had taken him back. "Oh, he begged her," a close friend of Esther Hartman said. "He didn't want to be alone, he said. He'd miss her pies. He'd miss her mashed potatoes." Hartman said he was through with Katherine Sunderman. He and his wife took a trip together to Arkansas. He no longer found reasons for being away from the farm all the time. Rodney and Rollyn Hartman allowed themselves to believe that some inexplicable chapter in their father's life might have finally ended. By autumn, Esther Hartman seemed more cheerful than she had been in years. She chatted away with friends about plans for a new garden and a new strawberry patch. Then, shortly after 3 A.M. on a stormy Saturday in September, Charles Orr, who is the ambulance driver in Aplington as well as the Hartmans' pastor, was awakened by a telephone call from Lawrence Hartman. "It's

Esther," Hartman said. Orr drove the ambulance to the Hartman farmhouse. Esther Hartman was dead.

She had bruises on her face and hands. All but one of her ribs had been broken, crushing her lungs and cutting off her ability to breathe. Lawrence Hartman said he had been out during the evening — at Katherine Sunderman's new apartment, not far from the Happy Chef, in Cedar Falls, as it turned out — and after his return had found his wife at the bottom of the basement steps, presumably the victim of a fall while carrying laundry on the stairs. Hartman seemed in sort of a daze. "Esther was good to me," he told Rick Penning, who was then a deputy and is now the sheriff of Grundy County. "She always baked me stuff — pies and stuff." His sons — and particularly Rodney — were in a state that seemed in danger of erupting into violence. As the farmhouse began to fill up that night with the sheriff's deputies and doctors and friends, some of the law-enforcement people spent part of their time making certain that Lawrence Hartman was not alone with his sons. "I finally asked the boys if they would go up to Rollyn's home and wait until we called them," William Marten, who was then the sheriff, has said. "Because I felt the situation was becoming out of hand." Before the boys left, though, Rollyn had made their feelings clear to his father. "Someday," he told Lawrence Hartman, "you'll burn in hell."

Around Christmastime of 1980, Lawrence Hartman was indicted for the murder of his wife — the first murder case in Grundy County in thirty years. A few months later, Rodney and Rollyn brought a wrongful-death suit against their father in civil court — a suit that was really about who would own Esther Hartman's share of the farm she had worked on for so long. To defend him against the murder charge, Hartman hired one of the best-known criminal lawyers in the state. (People in Grundy County, speculating about the fee that such a big-city lawyer might command, said, "There goes one farm right there.") It was nearly a year before Hartman was actually tried for murder. The defense argued, without much opposition, that Hartman could not get an impartial jury in Grundy County, and the trial was set for the seat of Black Hawk County — Waterloo, the city right next to Cedar Falls. A lot of people from Grundy County made the drive daily. At times, there were crowds too large to be accommodated in the courtroom. The atmosphere among the spectators was caught by a photograph in the *Des Moines Register* — a row of eight women, middle-aged or older, staring at the proceedings with expressions that carried no hint of forgiveness.

The prosecutor, a young Grundy Center attorney named Richard Pilcher, presented evidence to show that in the summer of 1980 Lawrence Hartman had gone back to Katherine Sunderman after all. He had given her a diamond ring. He had leased a car for her. He had promised her that once the fall harvest was in he would have his final divorce settlement and would then be able to marry her. They had talked about a honeymoon in Hawaii. Evidence was entered that Hartman had once injured his wife by kicking her, and that she had expressed fear that he would attack her again. Pilcher claimed that Hartman had wanted "the best of both worlds" — the pies and cakes and solidity of the home that Esther provided as well as a new and drastically different life with a cocktail waitress who had a habit of calling men "tiger." According to the prosecution's case, when Hartman finally had to make a choice — when he was getting pressure from Katherine Sunderman to marry her and getting pressure to straighten out from his wife and his sons and pressure from the court injunction — he saw no way to have both his farm and his new life except to kill Esther. Rodney and Rollyn both testified against their father.

"The truth of the matter is, Rollyn," the defense lawyer said on cross-examination, "you'd like to see him, in your words, 'burn in hell.'"

"Well, if that's justice," Rollyn said.

Hartman did not deny his relationship with Katherine Sunderman — that he had slept with her the night of Esther Hartman's death, that he had lied to his family about her, that he was living with her as he stood trial for his wife's murder, that he planned to marry her. Although he expressed his love for his wife ("Esther was a good person; nothing wrong with Esther"), he said that his marriage had dried up after the boys moved out. He had told Katherine Sunderman that he felt like a slave at times, and that Esther sometimes seemed to care more for her brothers than she did for him. Throughout the trial, it was said that Lawrence and Esther Hartman had become incompatible. The word used to describe the relationship between Lawrence Hartman and Katherine Sunderman was "bouncy" — in Katherine Sunderman's testimony, "very bouncy." There wasn't much brought out about Hartman's behavior that might have softened the stares of the women who drove to the courthouse from Grundy County every day. The defense attorney took care to remind the jury that "Lawrence Hartman isn't on trial here for having an affair."

To refute the testimony of pathologists called by the prosecution, the defense presented some pathologists who said that Esther Hartman's injuries could have resulted from a fall and an effort at cardiopulmonary resuscitation by her husband. Even so, there were a lot of problems with the defendant's explanation of what had happened that night. He had to explain what he was doing in the basement, and why Esther was walking back down the basement stairs with clean laundry of Rodney's that had been seen in the kitchen that afternoon, and why a couple of presumably disinterested neighbors testified that they had seen him in Aplington or Parkersburg when his alibi called for him to be in Cedar Falls. Katherine Sunderman's testimony supported Hartman's story — if that can be said of testimony that she knew he was still in her bed at two in the morning because she had set the alarm clock for two in order to take a twelve-hour cold pill — but she acknowledged making a statement that seemed rather damaging. When an investigator informed her that Esther Hartman was dead, Katherine Sunderman acknowledged, her response had been to blurt out, "Oh, God! Was she beaten?"

Pilcher asked the jury to find Hartman guilty of first-degree murder — murder committed with premeditation as well as intent. It may be that the prosecution itself had poked too many holes in Hartman's story to make premeditation plausible. If Hartman had planned the whole thing, the jurors may have surmised, wouldn't he have done a better job of tying up loose ends than that? They apparently believed, though, that Lawrence Hartman had killed his wife — killed her in a drunken rage, maybe, or killed her because he had started hitting her and couldn't stop. After eight and a half hours of deliberation, Hartman was found guilty of second-degree murder. The judge sentenced him to twenty-five years in prison.

Because the case was appealed to the Iowa Supreme Court, Lawrence Hartman was able to remain free on a hundred-thousand-dollar bond. A couple of months after the trial was over, he and Katherine Sunderman were married. They continue to live in the apartment that Hartman visited the night his wife died. They are not seen around northern Grundy County. For the most part, what Hartman's former neighbors know about him and his new wife is what they read in the papers. A recent item, reprinted in the Grundy County weekly from the Waterloo paper, reported that Katherine Sunderman Hartman had been picked up by the Iowa State Patrol for driving while intoxicated, and that Lawrence Hartman, who was in the car with her, was booked at the same time for public intoxication.

There are, of course, still a lot of different theories in Grundy County to account for how Lawrence Hartman was transformed from a pillar of the German farming community into a man who carried on with a cocktail waitress and lost the respect of his sons and was eventually convicted of murdering his own wife. Some people think that Hartman simply fell into bad company — high-steppers who exposed an unworldly farmer to temptations he couldn't resist. Some people think he just happened to be smitten — bewitched, maybe — by Katherine Sunderman. ("The defendant becomes obsessed with this other woman," Pilcher said in his closing statement. "He becomes totally dominated by this woman, and she gains control of his every action. She caused substantial changes in the defendant, in his personality and in his character. His association with her ruins his relationship with his wife and his two sons, Rodney and Rollyn.") In the Shamrock Café in Aplington not long ago, one man offered the possibility that Lawrence Hartman's change had been almost biological. "I heard that some men have a change of life, just like women," he said. "Their whole personality changes." The man across the booth shook his head, held up his hand, and rubbed his thumb and forefinger together. "Money," he said. "There are very few people who can stand being rich."

Rodney Hartman seems to share that interpretation, more or less. When asked what happened to his father, he says, "Inflation." He means inflation in land values. "All of a sudden, people were coming up to him and saying, 'Lawrence, you're rich,'" Rodney said recently. Even now, there are people in Grundy County who don't believe that Lawrence Hartman killed his wife, but his sons are not among them. They resent the fact that he is free — living with the woman they shouted at as a home-wrecker — even after a jury found him guilty of killing their mother. Rodney and Rollyn planted the Hartman acres in corn and beans this spring without the help of their father. Under an out-of-court settlement of the civil suit, the sons farm the Hartman land with the agreement that they pay their father a lump sum of more than two hundred thousand dollars, plus thirty thousand dollars a year for the next twenty years. Given the added burden, the younger Hartmans don't sound completely confident of being able to make a go of it, but they are obviously committed to trying. For some time after his mother's death, Rollyn couldn't bring himself to enter the farmhouse, but now he has plans to move there with his wife and child. It is, after all, the Hartman home place.

Afterword

"If he had come two weeks later, he would have written a different story," Keith Lingwall, pastor of the First Lutheran Church of Fairfield, Iowa, remarked some months after the piece I wrote about the death of So Yang appeared in *The New Yorker*. He made the remark as a way of expressing his belief that the tension the incident engendered between Baptists and other churchgoing Christians in Fairfield had subsided rather quickly — among the contentions made by Lynn Bergfalk of the First Baptist Church, who believed the piece had treated the Baptists unfairly, was that I had exaggerated or perhaps even invented the tension — but what Lingwall said could be applied in general to a lot of magazine pieces. A reporter tries to catch a story on some sort of plateau — the end of a phase, if not the end of the story — and which plateau it is tends to color his view of what happened. The bleak future facing the *Georgia Gazette* when I left Savannah was an element in a story that was partly about defying the customary way established families there sort out difficulties. A year and a half later, though, the designation as official forum for legal advertising was returned to the *Gazette,* and the Scardinos have since launched a second paper in the Savannah suburbs. A magazine piece doesn't present history; in a couple of weeks or a couple of years there is likely to be another plateau.

Waiting for the second of John Mervin's shooting trials before writing about his career as an undercover policeman wouldn't have changed the story at all: in 1970, a West Chester jury concluded that he was not guilty of assault with intent to kill when he shot Robert Miller in the back and the leg outside a West Chester tavern. A couple of years after that, though, the story changed drastically. The *Philadelphia Bulletin* reported that it had a sworn statement by Eugene Moran, whose apartment was the scene of Jonathan Henry's death, stating that Mervin had killed Henry in cold blood, that a West Chester policeman had helped rearrange the scene of the shooting before township police arrived, and that a number of witnesses had perjured themselves at the trial. That article, by Greg Walter, and the ones that followed it led to investigations of Mervin's trials and the circumstances of his employment as an undercover policeman. Eventually, Mervin, among others, was indicted on a number of charges. He was acquitted of most of them. Even after the time had passed when he could enter the courtroom as a certified battler against the forces corrupting our youth, Mervin remained a young man jurors tended to find impressive. "He has the face of a Hummell figurine," one attorney told the *Inquirer*. It wasn't quite enough. For persuading witnesses to lie on his behalf in the Miller trial, he was convicted of conspiracy and suborning perjury and given a sentence of three to seven years.

The killings that provoked mysteries tended to remain mysterious, still subject to the sort of speculation that I usually found more interesting than the answer to who done it. Two years after Harvey St. Jean was murdered, Gene Miller did a long piece in the *Miami Herald* on the police investigation; it was headlined "ST. JEAN DEATH: NEW FACTS AND NEW MYSTERIES." The police had come across all sorts of intriguing facts — a safety-deposit box stuffed with cash, some unsavory business associations, a claim against the estate by a Cuban gangster whose bond money St. Jean apparently had failed to return when it was due — but they didn't find out who shot Harvey St. Jean.

Some months after Theng Pao Yang had recovered from his suicide attempt, he tried to explain to a reporter why he had believed his entire family should take their lives, but the explanation sounded no more logical than the ones he had offered from his hospital bed. Although he didn't mention any threats from the lowland Laotians, he did say that he had believed his entire family was about to be killed. Because the incidents he mentioned as having led him to that conclusion were not the sort of incidents that ordinarily constitute grounds for mass murder in Iowa — he said, for instance, that the Yangs had disappointed others in the First Baptist congregation by failing to contribute at the Sunday offering — it was assumed that Yang's terrible decision had been brought about by paranoia or a communication problem or disorientation or "trauma syndrome" or a combination of all of them. As sudden deaths of Hmong refugees were going, it turned out, the death of So Yang was not particularly mysterious: by 1981, newspapers were reporting that as many as eighteen of the Hmong refugees who had emigrated to America had died in their sleep from no obvious cause — a phenomenon that was known as "bangungut," after the Filipino word for nightmare. When I read about bangungut, it occurred to me that just about every one of those eighteen deaths must have caused a number of fundamentally decent and generous-hearted sponsors of refugees to search for blame and try to apportion guilt — perhaps, as Barbara Hill told me in Fairfield, trying to find reasons for something the Hmong never intended there to be a reason for.

A solution was offered for the killing that had been the basis for the greatest variety of speculation — the mysterious death of Walter Bopp. About a year after I left Tucson, three men were charged with Bopp's murder. According to the police, Bopp had indeed been a hoarder of silver — silver accumulated over years of thrifty living rather than silver witched from the Southern Arizona desert — and had died because of it. Authorities said that at least two hundred thousand

Afterword

dollars' worth of silver bars and jewelry had been stolen from Bopp, and that the men who tortured him in the back of his store were trying to find out where to get more. Some of the mystery of why he remained silent about the identity of his attackers may have been cleared up by the fact that one of the three accused men was Jerry Gilligan — a son of Bopp's second wife, the soothsayer. Gilligan was still at large a year later when the other two men charged in the case pleaded guilty to second-degree murder.

For some time, the story of the feud in Riverside, California, seemed to be on an endless plateau of violence. In 1980, three people were killed in the feud, two of them within the same week in the same Casa Blanca front yard. There came a time, apparently, when the nighttime gunfire in Casa Blanca was so heavy that some residents felt the need to sleep in their bathtubs for protection. Then, after a while, Casa Blanca became a lot quieter. The calm was attributed to a number of factors — a police task force that had been sent in after the two people were killed in one week, the sobering effect of the first murder conviction since the beginning of the feud, or maybe just the fact that a lot of the most intense participants were temporarily behind bars. "It's really calmed down a lot," a Casa Blanca resident told James Richardson of the *Press-Enterprise.* "But it will come back up again. It just will. If you've lived here before, you'd know about it." It was just another way of telling a reporter that if he came back in two weeks he would probably write a different story.